Faith for a New Day

Faith for a New Day

The New View of the Gospel of John

by Lamar Cope

CBP Press
St. Louis, Missouri

Unless otherwise indicated, all scripture quotations are from the
Revised Standard Version of the Bible, copyrighted 1946, 1952, ©
1971, 1973, by the Division of Christian Education of the National
Council of the Churches of Christ in the United States of America,
and are used by permission.

Library of Congress Cataloging-in-Publication Data

Cope, Lamar.
    Faith for a new day.

    Bibliography: p. 115
    Includes index.
    1. Bible. N.T. John—Criticism, interpretation, etc. I. Title.
BS2615.2.C68   1986   226'.506   86-6131
ISBN 0-8272-1013-2

Foreword

In 1960 the Southern novelist Flannery O'Connor said that while the South is "hardly Christ-centered, it is most certainly Christ-haunted" (*Mystery and Manners*, p. 44). Now, after a quarter of a century, one can say something similar about virtually the whole of American culture: While it is scarcely Bible-centered, it is surely Bible-haunted. Being, as it were, a group of sailors cast adrift on a tempestuous and threatening cosmic sea, we suspect that the Bible may contain, or somehow refer to, our only sure compass. At the same time, however, we have grown very suspicious of those who call upon the Bible most loudly and most publicly in a highly simplistic fashion. As a result we often fall into a state of profound ambivalence. Upon reflection, we notice that we even transfer that ambivalence to the Bible itself, considering it to be filled with *promise*, and equally, or nearly equally, filled with *problems*. In a word, we find the Bible to be like the proverbial spouse: hard to live with and impossible to live without.

In the book that now lies in our hands, Lamar Cope faces this profound ambivalence head-on; and with his characteristic wisdom, he chooses to explore it by taking up a single book of the Bible, the beautiful and majestic, the earthy and mysterious Gospel of John. Fully abreast of contemporary research, Cope shares with us not only its best results, but also his own seasoned interpretation. Moreover, we are treated to his truly remarkable gifts as a pedagogue. We learn. The result is that we are taken into new territory, where, by noting how John brought the inherited portrait of Jesus into vital relationship with the problems and challenges of his own time and setting (near the close of the first century), we can be encouraged to do the same vis-à-vis our own time and setting. For, as Cope clearly says, the vexing and complex problems of our new day are in fact related to Jesus Christ. For that reason our call is to do in our own setting nothing less than the work of the One who sent Jesus (John 9:4 and 14:12). It is a very tall order, one that is possible only with the guidance of the Paraclete and with the help of books such as the one now in our hands.

J. Louis Martyn
Edward Robinson Professor of Biblical Theology
Union Theological Seminary

Preface

The story of this book's writing is almost as complex as that of its subject, the Gospel of John. It was begun several years ago at the request of a former editor of Bethany Press, the parent of CBP Press. It began as a study on a single theme, the sending motif in the Gospel. But as I worked with adult study groups throughout the southeastern Wisconsin area, it became clear that most readers were unaware of the dramatic changes in our view of the Fourth Gospel that have come about since 1945.

So the study shifted to a general introduction to the gospel's story seen in this new way. The pressures of a college teaching load slowed its completion until, in the winter of 1983, I had an opportunity to teach a term as a visiting professor at United Theological College in Bangalore, South India. There, on a borrowed typewriter, and on dubious quality paper, a draft was completed. It arrived just as Bethany Press suspended publication. Retyped and recirculated, it sought another publishing home unsuccessfully. Then, in the fall of 1985, just as I was about to scuttle or drastically revise the project, it was sent one last time to Bethany, now CBP Press. There it has received enthusiastic support from Editor Herb Lambert, and so *Faith for a New Day* is born.

Over those years thanks are due to many individuals and institutions for support, assistance, and encouragement. Southern Methodist University, Garrett-Evangelical Seminary, Nashotoh House Seminary and, of course, Carroll College have been supportive in library facilities and broad encouragement. This note is tinged with sadness in acknowledging that the typing in India was done on the typewriter of the late Frank Collison, whose friendship and support I prized and whose recent untimely death is a blow to all New Testament studies and to the world church. Thanks are also due to Sandi Wright, whose careful overtime typing greatly improved the final manuscript; to my Carroll student secretary, Cathy Trelka, for work on the indexes; and to a number of others whose help has made the book possible.

But most of all the readers should know that here a debt is partially paid to several great teachers who have shared their love of John's Gospel with me. They are Peder Borgen, Oscar Cullmann, Raymond Brown, Robert Fortna and J. Louis Martyn. That I was able to know or study with these scholars is a rare privilege. So, while they are not to blame for the errors in this overview of the Fourth Gospel, there is no question that their learning and their love for the Fourth Gospel are the well from which this book is drawn.

Lamar Cope
Carroll College
Waukesha, WI
March 1986

Contents

Introduction

We are living in a time of renewed religious concern in the United States. Perhaps it is no more than one of the recurrent tides of revival and renewal that have always marked U.S. religious life. However, unlike the renewal of the late forties and early fifties, this one is occurring in a time of deep uncertainty. Those earlier days were times of optimism and confidence in the future. These are "down" times, times of foreboding. The nearly frantic spasms of the sixties and seventies, with their exultant call for social change and for the demolition of outworn beliefs and values, seem to have left us spiritually dry and rootless and set the stage for a reappraisal of the role of religion in life. However historians or sociologists may analyze the causes, we are experiencing a renewed quest for stable religious beliefs, norms and anchors in our society today.

The role of the Bible in that quest is a remarkable one. In case after case, Christians seeking those anchors have turned to a biblical faith as the way for today. All of us are aware of the rapid growth of "Bible Christianity" and of the resurgence of fundamentalism in both theology and scriptural interpretation. The Moral Majority movement, the great popularity of Billy Graham and television programs such as the *700 Club* all are examples of this turning to the Bible for answers to modern religious problems. This "turn to the Bible" is happening in spite of the extreme difficulties such biblicism has in dealing with modern life.

There is, of course, the obvious clash between modern science and a literalist view of the Bible. And even though it is a battle that the literalist cannot ultimately win (for the nuclear, space and RNA/DNA discoveries are here to stay), sincere people nevertheless choose to claim literal belief in the Bible in order to have an anchor in today's confusing world. Then, too, there is the problem of the dependency of parts of the Bible's message on ancient culture. Biblical attitudes toward slavery, the roles of men and women, divorce and sexuality are rooted in those cultures of thousands of years ago and are impossible to practice today in good conscience. So literalists often choose to adapt what they like and ignore what they cannot adapt on these subjects.

It is easy for secular and liberal critics to scoff at the Bible pounders and their unreasonable stance. But it is much more difficult to point to a better way which honors the biblical and Christian heritage, without being narrow-minded, defensive and even arrogant. It is the purpose of this study to probe a possible better way by asking the reader to share in a new view of the New Testament materials as exemplified in contemporary research on the Gospel of John, and to ask how this new view may throw light on our being Christian today.

1

How the Fourth Gospel Came to Be

Throughout this century, but especially since 1945, a series of excellent scholarly works has been unraveling the secrets of the book called the Gospel of John. Some of the most important aids in this discovery were external evidences. A manuscript was discovered that can be dated around A.D. 125-150, which puts to rest any claims that this Gospel is a very late Gentile work. Better analysis of the available Jewish sources, as with other New Testament studies, has helped us to understand the relationship between the Christian documents and their Jewish environment. Especially helpful has been the evidence of the expulsion of Christians from the Jewish synagogues in the late first century, for that helps locate in concrete historical events the comments on synagogue expulsion that are found in John 9, 12, and 16.

Before looking at those results it is important to rethink what a "gospel" is. Familiarity with the Christian Gospels is great among Christians and this may seem like an absurd suggestion. But this familiarity often keeps readers from seeing what is there. The Gospels are often viewed as historical biographies of Jesus of Nazareth. Often, the Four Gospels included in the New Testament are combined into one amalgamated, or harmonized, story. A more careful look shows that such harmonization is impossible because the Gospels differ greatly from one another both in scope and in specific details. Moreover, the more careful look would also show that the starting premise is wrong. The Gospels are not, and were never intended to be, the historical biographies that moderns have expected them to be.

Although all of these books, in the earliest available manuscripts, were untitled and anonymous, the term gospel was quickly applied to them in the second century church. The word *gospel* (from the Greek *euaggelion*) means "announced good news." This ancient title goes a long way toward helping to understand what the books are. They are announcements of the good news about Jesus the crucified and risen Lord. They are primarily affirmations of faith. But they are more than that. Each of the canonical Gospels, as well as some of the noncanonical ones, was penned by an early Christian with an urgent message for a particular situation. For that reason, all the Gospels are just as directed toward their intended readers as are the obviously situational letters of Paul. Each Gospel represents first and foremost that writer's proclamation about the meaning of Christian faith for that time, for those people, in that place. Only indirectly and, one must add, fortunately, are there genuine historical reminiscences embedded in these faith documents.

With this understanding of the Gospels, sense can be made of their sharply differing content, their different emphases and their uniqueness. This allows the Gospels to tell their story. It is this shift in emphasis that the study of the Gospel of John requires. For two hundred years scholars have been fascinated with the task of discovering the historical Jesus behind the Gospels, what he did and what he *really* said. Viewed in that way, John has been thought to be of little value (although even that is changing today). But the primary point of a gospel as Gospel is the story of a writer and a community's faith. In a concern to peel away additions and get back to Jesus, something precious is peeled away. Hence, recent Gospel criticism has shifted our focus to the stories of the development of the Gospels and to the message of the Gospels themselves. Here is an opportunity to witness early Christians—indeed, some of the earliest Christians—struggling with the same question that haunts Christians today, "What does it mean to be Christian in our time?"

Modern historical scholarship is in general agreement about the stages in the development of the work called John. At the base of this document lies a very early "Signs Gospel." That is, very early in the life of the community from which our book comes, a Christian wrote a book proclaiming faith in Jesus the Messiah who performed signs to prove his Messiahship. A number of clues can be detected to show that this book was used as a basis for the Gospel of John. First, in John 2:11 and 4:54 the two miracles associated with Cana are counted as the first and second signs that Jesus performed. But the most telling evidence is in the concluding sentences of chapter 20: "Now Jesus did many other signs in the presence of the disciples, which are not written in this book; but *these* [italics added] are written that you may believe that Jesus is the Christ . . ."(vs. 30-31). By no stretch of the imagination could a reader describe the present Gospel of John as a book of signs, yet here is a conclusion to just such a book. It seems almost inescapable that the book read today as John is based on an earlier gospel revered by that Christian community. The present book does not consider a faith based solely on signs to be a mature faith. (See especially the experience of the blind man in chapter 9.)

Moreover, the miracle stories in John are units in themselves, differing from the material around them in vocabulary and style, and at times awkwardly connected to their contexts or interrupted by explanatory asides (e.g., 9:4). Thus, while it is uncertain what the original Signs Gospel contained or whether every Johannine miracle story derived from it, it is clear that originally a gospel of signs had been written for this Christian community.

For a time that gospel must have served well the Christian Jews who made up the community. But after the wrenching disaster of the Jewish War of A.D. 66-70 and its aftermath, the Signs Gospel became out-of-date. So, in the decades A.D. 80-100 another Christian writer undertook a revision of the Gospel for that new day. It is this author who added the brilliant "I am" discourses and the extensive dialogues with opponents that now dominate this Gospel. It is this writer who is called the Evangelist John or the Fourth Evangelist. As will be illustrated, he took the community's cherished Signs Gospel and gave it a new shape, a new meaning, one which fit their changed situation. Exact limits between the Signs Gospel and the revision are sometimes blurred, but a reader can usually distinguish the two strands by simply marking off the miracle story proper from its surrounding context, a dialogue or sermon by Jesus, and thus see the work of the great evangelist-editor called John. Most critics believe that John chose the hymn/poem in 1:1-18 called the prologue, revised it to make it fit his purpose and Christology, and used it to preface his work. In doing so, he set the tone for the revised Gospel and introduced a number of themes important to the rest of the story.

But the development was not yet finished. The reader will note that chapter 21 seems to be an appendix that has been added to the work. Even without the technical evidence that the vocabulary and style are new and different, the addition is evident in the closing verses.

This is the disciple who is bearing witness to these things, and who has written these things; and we know that his testimony is true (21:24).

This comment about the beloved disciple of the story just completed is clearly in the first-person plural yet it is written about the disciple in third person. He could not have written those lines. The whole chapter reads as an add-on to the conclusion in 20:30-31. The stories of chapter 21 are located in Galilee and not in Jerusalem, as are the stories of chapter 20. It is an unmistakable later appendix to the Gospel. Many critics also think that chapters 15 and 16 were added to the final discourse at this time.

There are more complicated analyses of the Fourth Gospel than this three-stage approach, but their very complexity makes them suspect. In any case, it is clear that the Gospel read today is the final product of at least a three-step development as the Gospel was adapted to the needs of a living Christian community. So, too, its message is forged by the experiences of these Christians and by the genius of its author/editors. Here is a document which began as a simple Signs Gospel, was revised for a new day by a later evangelist, and then finally was amended by the addition of chapters 15, 16 and 21.

Suggested Supplementary Reading
The best commentary is that of R. E. Brown in the *Anchor Bible*, Vols. 29 and 29a (New York: Doubleday, 1966, 1970). It gives extensive treatment of the questions of sources, authorship and date. Brown's own theory of composition in five stages is extremely complex, however.

An invaluable resource is the survey by Robert Kysar, *The Fourth Evangelist and His Gospel: An Examination of Contemporary Scholarship* (Minneapolis: Augsburg, 1975). Also valuable is his study book, *John, the Maverick Gospel* (Atlanta: John Knox, 1976).

Readers who wish to see a technical analysis of the Signs Gospel and proposed Greek text should consult R.T. Fortna, *The Gospel of Signs* (Cambridge, 1970).

Questions and Suggestions for Study

1. Examine John 2:11, 4:54 and 20:30-31. Do you see the evidence for an earlier book? Why are the miracles numbered? Does the end of chapter 20 characterize the present Gospel?

2. Using a concordance, look up some key words of the prologue (1:1-18) such as light, darkness, truth. How do they reoccur in the dialogues and discourses?

3. Compare chapters 20 and 21. What are some reasons why the last chapter is an appendix?

4. What does the discovery of the steps in the construction of this Gospel mean to you as you think about the Gospel? How is it troubling? helpful?

In Beginning:
The Signs Gospel Faith

"In beginning" is a literal translation of the first two words of the Gospel of John. The earliest stages of the Gospel's story are, of course, the years of the oral tradition, when the community carried on its life and mission with no written texts. As shown in both Acts and the letters of Paul, Christians quickly began spreading the good news in Palestine and Syria, primarily among Jewish people. Somewhere in northern Palestine or southern Syria a particular kind of Christian movement began to form that traced its origins to the preaching of the "beloved disciple." Who that person was is uncertain. Later tradition identifies him as John Zebedee, hence the Gospel's name.

Internal evidence may point more clearly to Lazarus, over whom "Jesus wept" (John 11:35), or it may be an early disciple unknown to us by name.

Either that disciple, or the leader of the community that he helped form, struck upon the idea of a book which would aid in their testimony to the faith. Its outline was simple. Jesus was shown to be the true Messiah by a recounting of his signs or mighty deeds or wonders. Robert Fortna thinks that there were probably seven signs climaxed by the greatest wonder of all, the cross and resurrection. (See his book, *The Gospel of Signs.*) The recounting was probably introduced by a brief narrative, now imbedded in 1:19-42, which showed the reader how far superior Jesus was to John the Baptist.

The signs, or miracle stories, were simply told in this early Gospel. A good illustration of this is the first sign, the changing of water into wine at the wedding of Cana.

> On the third day there was a marriage at Cana in Galilee, and the mother of Jesus was there; Jesus also was invited to the marriage, with his disciples. When the wine gave out, the mother of Jesus said to him, "They have no wine." And Jesus said to her, "O woman, what have you to do with me? My hour has not yet come." His mother said to the servants, "Do whatever he tells you." Now six stone jars were standing there, for the Jewish rites of purification, each holding twenty or thirty gallons. Jesus said to them, "Fill the jars with water." And they filled them up to the brim. He said to them, "Now draw some out, and take it to the steward of the feast." So they took it. When the steward of the feast tasted the water now become wine, and did not know where it came from (though the servants who had drawn the water knew), the steward of the feast called the bridegroom and said to him, "Every man serves the good wine first; and when men have drunk freely, then the poor wine; but you have kept the good wine until now." This, the first of his signs, Jesus did at Cana in Galilee, and manifested his glory; and his disciples believed in him (2:1-11).

Here is a simple dramatic narrative. The only intrusions of a later hand are the extraneous reply of Jesus to his mother in verse 4 and perhaps the parenthetical aside in verse 9. The account tells the story of the incident, with no subsequent explanation and no debate. It is simply "the first of his signs, [which] Jesus did at Cana in Galilee." In that light the conclusion in 20:30-31 makes perfect sense: "Now Jesus did many other signs ... which are not written in this book, but these are written that you may believe that Jesus is the Christ, the Son of God. . . ." In the primitive Signs Gospel a selection of the miracles of Jesus was offered as a testimony to his Messiahship.

That such an early Christian Jewish document existed is virtually certain. Why was the Christian story presented in this way? What assumptions guided the readers *and* the writer? Answers to those questions lead to an understanding of the faith of this early Christian community.

The Signs Gospel began with a denial of the importance of John the Baptist. That is a far cry from the honored place he holds in the opening verses of Mark as the forerunner of the Messiah (Mark 1:1-8). The reasons for this striking difference must lie in the situation faced by the community for which the Signs Gospel was written. They must have been in competition with the followers of John the Baptist. Contrary to the impression given in the Synoptic Gospels, the followers of John did not disappear after his execution by Herod Antipas. Instead, they continued as a religious community which revered John as God's true messenger, the "light" and the "truth." Elements of this John the Baptist community, though greatly changed by the tides of the centuries, survive to the present in the small Mandaean community of modern Iraq. These followers of John the Baptist were competitors with the community of the Signs Gospel in the spreading of their respective faiths. Small wonder, then, that the Christian Jews of this circle would want a testimony which refuted the claims of the followers of the Baptist. For example, "I baptize with water; but among you stands one whom you do not know, even he who comes after me, the thong of whose sandal I am not worthy to untie" (John 1:26-27). This Gospel does not even have an actual baptism of

Jesus by John, so strong is the aversion to making Jesus in any way subordinate to John.

The other key feature of the Signs Gospel is more puzzling. It is difficult to imagine a Christian Gospel that gives no account at all of Jesus' teaching, has practically no concern for chronology, and does not even tell the reader why the signs are of such importance. This bewilderment suggests that there was a tacit assumption on the part of the writer and his intended readers that answered these objections. That assumption had to be an expectation that when the Messiah appeared he would perform signs and be recognized by them.

Because the performance of signs and wonders is not a standard part of the Jewish Messianic hope, it has been important to find a background suitable for the assumption about signs that guided the Signs Gospel. A number of scholars, but especially Wayne Meeks in *The Prophet King*, have helped to discover a Jewish background for the signs tradition. In the century before Jesus, in some circles and especially in Galilee, the hopes for a Davidic royal warrior Messiah who would lead the people to victory and restoration had been complemented by a hope for a Messiah with the traits of a Mosaic prophet. That hope is rooted in the promise of Deuteronomy 18:15, "The LORD your God will raise up for you a prophet like me from among you, from your brethren—him you shall heed." In some Jewish circles where the two hopes had come together, the Davidic king and prophet like Moses, the expectation of the Messiah had been expanded and enriched.

What would be the main characteristics of a messiah who would be a prophet like Moses? Most Christians automatically think of Moses' role as lawgiver. But that is not the only side of the Moses story. Not only in the Old Testament, but also in the free oral tradition known as *Haggadah*, the remarkable feats of Moses as wonder worker were extolled. It was Moses who, at God's bidding and by God's power, unleashed the plagues on Egypt. It was Moses who held up his staff and parted the Red Sea. It was Moses' staff that banished the snakes in the wilderness; Moses who struck the rock and brought forth water; Moses who called on God and received manna from heaven. The promised messiah/prophet, like Moses, would also do such signs and wonders, and they would be a testimony to his identity. It was precisely that hope which the writer of the Signs Gospel addressed and relied upon.

Although it is the most dramatic and complete, this is not the only instance of the early Christians' use of Moses expectations in proclaiming Jesus to be the Messiah. In Peter's Pentecost sermon in Acts 2, a clear use of this tradition is encountered: "Men of Israel, hear these words: Jesus of Nazareth, a man attested to you by God with mighty works and wonders and signs which God did through him in your midst..." (v. 22). The Gospel of Matthew also stresses the Mosaic parallel. Jesus in the birth narratives flees to Egypt to escape a despot's wrath. The new law is given from the mountain. And the transfiguration story, older than any of the Gospels in oral tradition, echoes the Deuteronomic promise, "Him you shall heed," by turning it into a command as the voice from the cloud (cf. Exodus 34:5) said, "This is my beloved Son, with whom I am well pleased; *listen to him*" (Matthew 17:5, italics added).

That there had been a miracle tradition about Jesus from the beginning seems a certain result of form criticism's tracing of the Gospel stories' origins. How much or how little, if any, of this actually goes back to Jesus himself is still debated. However, most critics today would concede that, at the very least, Jesus had the power of faith healing and exorcism to some degree (as did many others in the first century, Rabbi Jochanan ben Zakkai among them). It is also clear that the miraculous side of the Jesus story was greatly expanded in the telling and preaching of the first few decades. So the raw material of stories of Jesus' "mighty works and wonders and signs" were readily available to the Signs Gospel author.

The author of this early Gospel set out to provide a book that would make explicit the Christian claim to the Messiahship of Jesus by pointing the reader to Jesus' mighty works, those of a prophet like Moses. From the stories about Jesus that were circulating in the Christian community he selected a few to make the case. The old conclusion in 20:30 points to that selection with the words, "Now Jesus did many other signs. . . ." The uniqueness of the Christian tradition of this community is clear in the choices made. There are stories similar to the healing of the official's son at Capernaum, the feeding of the 5,000 and the walking on the water in the Synoptic Gospel accounts. But the wedding at Cana, the healing of the paralytic at Bethzatha pool, the healing of the blind man and the raising of Lazarus have no real counterparts in the Synoptic tradition. That suggests that the author's source for these stories is the community's oral tradition. They were the result of the remembering, revising and creating activity of this portion of the early church, quite different from the Palestinian Christian tradition behind the Synoptic Gospels.

At first sight that conclusion seems odd. Does it mean that in only twenty years the Christian movement had diversified so much? Yes, it had diversified that quickly. Already in the forties there was a well-defined Christian community centered in Jerusalem of a different sort than those in Samaria, Damascus and Antioch. Those communities' roots were in Greek-speaking Diaspora Judaism and they were less Torah (law)-conscious, less intensely apocalyptic than the Jerusalem Christians. Moreover, Paul had begun a vigorous campaign to form an almost entirely Gentile church tradition from northern Syria to Macedonia. So the evidence is clear that there was a great deal of diversity, very early, in the expressions of the Christian faith in Jesus as crucified and risen Messiah/Lord. The Signs Gospel is another window into the variety of earliest Christian faith. Whatever else that community believed, and guesses are all that can be made, they clearly believed that it was possible to portray Jesus to their fellow Jews as the promised Messiah/prophet like Moses.

This then was a major element in the mission preaching and faith of the Signs Gospel community. The document must have won strong approval and have become a standard for their way of expressing Christian faith. In those first few decades of the faith, the simple proclamation of Jesus the wonder-working Messiah/prophet like Moses was adequate both as a means of promoting the faith and for understanding it. But stormier days were on the horizon.

Suggested Supplementary Reading

A detailed discussion of the Mosaic-prophet expectation is found in W. Meeks, *The Prophet King* (Leiden: E.J. Brill, 1967).

J. L. Martyn provides a similar picture of this earliest stage in *The Gospel of John in Christian History* (New York: Paulist Press, 1978), pp. 93-102.

See also R. Kysar, *John, the Maverick Gospel.*

Questions and Suggestions for Study

1. According to Fortna there were seven signs in the Signs Gospel; can you find them?

2. Check the parallel accounts of the miracle stories in the other Gospels using the references your Bible provides. What miracles in John are independent?

3. Notice that the writer and the readers seem to have shared an unquestioning belief in miracles. Does that trouble you? Why or why not?

3

The Dark Interlude:
The Jewish War of A.D. 66-73
and Its Aftermath

The tragic events of the sixties and seventies of the first
Christian century completely recast the lives and fortunes of
Christians and Jews, not just in Palestine but throughout the
Roman Empire. It was an upheaval that had been a long time
brewing, resulting in a bloodbath that darkened the land,
impoverished the people, destroyed villages and cities, and left
the Jewish people in turmoil and defeat.

During, and even before, the time of Jesus' ministry there had been a growing militant opposition to Roman rule by Jewish partisans. To them it mattered little that the Romans had been invited into the country by a populace weary of the tyranny of the last Maccabean (Jewish) kings. What did matter was that a foreign, pagan power ruled in the land that by God's promise belonged to the children of the covenant. And although the Romans were no more and no less harsh in dealing with their Jewish subjects than with others, their taxation was heavy and their administration of justice often cruel.

Rome had been wise enough not to force its pantheon of gods upon the Jews. A special pact had made Judaism an exception, a *religio licitia*, with its followers having the right not to worship the Roman gods. But in the years A.D. 30-65 that exception was threatened once by Caligula and again by Nero, so that fervently patriotic Jews felt no security in the Roman exception. The Zealots, as the partisans were called, grew in strength almost in tandem with the ineptness of the administration of Judea and Galilee by the Roman procurators. The Zealots were particularly conscious of those Jews who collaborated with the enemy; they harassed and even assassinated some of these persons, and swore vengeance when the revolution came. When and where possible the Zealots made a concerted effort to force Jews to cut all dealings with Rome.

The Christian Jewish communities found themselves caught up in this turmoil. As pacifists they refused to join the Zealot campaign. Insofar as most of them were faithful, Torah-keeping Jews who believed in Jesus the Messiah, they were able to stand apart. But there was pressure created by the acceptance of non-Jews into Christian circles outside Palestine. However blurred it may be by Luke's editorial hand, the story of Paul's last visit to Jerusalem is one overshadowed by partisan Jewish outrage at his law-free version of Gentile Christianity. A few years earlier James, the brother of Jesus and the leader of the Jerusalem Christians, was stoned to death by what was likely a Zealot-inspired mob seeking to force Christian Jews into greater orthodoxy. These were troubled times.

Then in A.D. 66, the country burst into open flame over a minor incident at Caesarea. Quickly the Roman garrisons were driven from Galilee by the rebels. Finally even the citadel in Jerusalem fell and its Roman force was slaughtered. Israel had rid itself of the Roman yoke. In those early days of the war it must have seemed that once again, as in the days of the Judges and the Maccabean revolt, a Jewish army had put to rout a vastly superior military force. Yahweh had again redeemed his people.

But after the first blush of success, cold reality reasserted itself. Rival Zealot parties struggled for leadership of the new Jewish state and the hostilities broke into open warfare and treachery. Slowly, methodically, the Roman general Vespasian set out to reconquer the rebellious territory. He recaptured Galilee and cut off access to Jerusalem in A.D. 68. Then he patiently rooted out all signs of rebellion in the Judean countryside. It was in this year that the sectarian community at Qumran was taken and burned. Then the Roman forces, now led by Titus who had taken command when his father returned to Rome to become emperor, completely encircled Jerusalem. After a long siege which reduced the population to near starvation, a Roman assault succeeded in breaching the city wall and reconquering the city. In the melee, the temple was accidentally set afire. The Romans leveled the city wall and burned and looted the city. The Arch of Titus in Rome shows him and his legions returning in a victory parade from Jerusalem with the looted spoils of the temple and the Jewish captives. The rebellion had failed!

The last desperate flicker was quenched in the spring of A.D. 73 when the heroic, but now pathetic, Zealot defenders of the remote desert fortress of Masada committed suicide rather than fall into enemy hands. In the aftermath of the rebellion, the country lay in ruins. Thousands of Jews had died in the fighting, killed by either the Romans, the Zealots, or the famine of besieged cities. Thousands more had been enslaved by the Romans in reprisal. Whole villages and cities lay in ruins, Jerusalem above all. The cherished temple, center of the Jewish religious cultus, was a heap of rubble and Jews were forbidden to enter the area. It is nearly impossible to imagine the shock and pain and dislocation the spasm of rebellion against Rome had caused. For Jews of every sort it was devastating.

Before the revolt Judaism had been a lively and diverse religious community. Sadducees, Pharisees, Essenes, Hellenistic and Christian Jews had all been involved in an intra-community debate about the most correct way to be Jewish. No one group, or two groups, held a powerful upper hand. Though the Jewish court was dominated by the Sadducees, its power lay primarily in making decisions related to the cult, the calendar, and feasts. When the rubble of the war began to clear, however, all of that was changed. The Essenes had been routed from their communities on the fringe of society and their settlements destroyed. The Zealots had brought a shameful, stunning defeat upon the nation and were largely discredited. With the destruction of the temple, the Sadducees' reason for existence was wiped away. For all practical purposes all that was left in the ravished world of Judaism in Palestine were Pharisaic Jews and Christian Jews, plus a few smaller sects, such as the followers of John the Baptist.

Now these two groups became locked in a struggle over the remnant of Judaism. Who represents the true Israel, the true Judaism—Pharisees or Christians? It was a fateful struggle in many ways, for it helped shape the future of Western religion—both Jewish and Christian. Fifty years after the fall of Jerusalem, Pharisaism had extended its sway over virtually all of Judaism, and all opposition, including the Christian Jews, had been swept aside. Thus, today all branches of Judaism trace their roots to the Pharisaism, known as Tannaitic, that rose from the fall of A.D. 70 to redirect, reunite and preserve Jewish faith and community in the Roman Empire. Its center of learning and power was the Academy at Jamnia, which had been established by Rabbi Johanan ben Zakkai even as the war was ending. It was made a power center by his successor,

Gamaliel the Second, head of the academy from A.D. 80-115.

Both the Gospel of Matthew and the Fourth Evangelist's revision of the Signs Gospel were written during the struggle for identity between Pharisaic and Christian Judaism. In large part that accounts for the bitter denunciations of the Pharisees and Jews, for in their world the Pharisees were the only significant Jewish opponents. The tensions of this period probably also account for the Talmudic traditions that are negative about Jesus, even though the Pharisees by and large ignored the groups they expelled.

So to understand John and his thought at all, the difficulties of his Christian Jewish community following the Jewish War must be understood. More and more, Jamnia Pharisaism sought to extend its sway over Jewish synagogues, seeking to exclude those Jews who did not keep Torah in their way. Exclusion from the synagogues was a far more serious punishment for a Jew than a modern Christian's expulsion from a church. The synagogue had become not just the religious but also the social unit of Judaism. Especially after A.D. 70, without the temple to provide a kind of center of orbit for Jewish life, it was the synagogue which filled that lack. Excluded persons were effectively shut off from the entire life of the community. No one would speak to them, not even members of their own family. No one would do business with them. Such a break was drastic and devastating.

Yet the Christians who formed the community of the Signs Gospel had lived all of their lives secure in a fundamentally Jewish identity. For them Jesus was the promised Messiah. Like the Matthean community, and the earliest church in Jerusalem, they had lived *as faithful Jews* who were *also* Christians. Now they found themselves more and more unwelcome, ousted and shunned by the synagogues as heretics, separated from the community that had always shaped their lives. This had to be a traumatic experience that produced a profound identity crisis. How could they, children of Abraham, followers of Moses and believers in Jesus the Messiah, accept their banishment from Judaism? The conflict separated families and tore apart communities (see Matthew 10:21-23, 34-39) and in some instances may have resulted in death for the heretic Christians. They were cut adrift and new answers were urgently needed.

The story of the actual breaking point emerges, most scholars today believe, in the period when Gamaliel II was head of the Academy of Jamnia. That group had become powerful enough to take the place of the old Sanhedrin of Jerusalem. Gamaliel is said to have asked his scholars to provide a way to oust the heretics from the synagogues. Rabbi Samuel the Small came up with the device. In every synagogue service there was a point, a high point, when an adult layman was called upon to recite the Eighteen Benedictions or Blessings. Samuel suggested the addition to the twelfth of these blessings, which already dealt with apostates, the words, "Let the Nazarenes and the Minim [heretics] be destroyed in a moment, and let them be blotted out of the Book of Life and not be inscribed together with the righteous."[1] When a Christian refused to say these damning lines, he was detected and expelled from the community.

With the enactment of that ruling and its enforcement in the synagogues, the die was finally cast. Though some Christians attempted to lead double lives and avoid detection (see John 12:42-43), for the most part the Christian Jewish community experienced wrenching separation from the synagogue world. The smoldering feud had led to complete separation. That the Johannine community was living through that time is unmistakable. So the Gospel can say, "For the Jews had already agreed that if any one should confess him to be Christ, he was to be put out of the synagogue" (9:22). It was to deal with the faith crisis which this separation caused that the Fourth Evangelist set out to revise the revered Signs Gospel.

Suggested Supplementary Reading

The best account of the process of separation of church and synagogue is in the work by J. L. Martyn cited above, *History and Theology in the Fourth Gospel* (Abingdon, 1979).

The primary source for information on the Jewish War is the work of the turncoat Jewish/Roman historian Josephus, *The Jewish War*, available in several editions.

For reading about the war and a classic story of an archeological expedition see Yigal Yadin, *Masada* (New York: Random, 1966). The reader should be aware, however, that the Zealots are somewhat idealized in this treatment.

Questions and Thoughts for Discussion

1. What might have happened in Western history if Christianity had remained a Jewish sect? How much influence, for good and ill, did this fateful separation have?

2. Read Matthew 23 in light of the evidence presented in this chapter. Do you think this denunciation reflects the attitude of Jesus, or of someone involved in the later conflict between Christians and Pharisees? Why?

4

John Revises the Signs Gospel for the New Day

The message of the Gospel of John as it appears today is not the product of the early Signs Gospel writer with minor changes, nor has its message been deeply affected by the later additions (e.g., chapter 21). The message of the Fourth Gospel is first and foremost the message of the Evangelist who recast the Signs Gospel into a stirring message of faith for his Christian community as it faced a perilous new time. Whoever this anonymous Christian thinker was, the brilliance of his work has sparked great faith, ideas and controversy ever since it was written. It is this great early Christian theologian who is meant when people speak today of John or the Fourth Evangelist.

The Community's Dilemma

When the Christian community that revered the Signs Gospel found itself faced with expulsion from the synagogue by the victorious Pharisees, its very faith was called into question. Never before had its sense of purpose and community identity been so sharply challenged. Part of the threat was social. When these persons were expelled from the synagogue by Judaism, they were thrown into a religious "no man's land" in the Roman world. Up until now they had lived under the aegis of the Roman recognition of Jewish religion (the war notwithstanding, although the temple tax was now paid directly to Rome). Cast out, they were nothing. Their allegiance to Jesus was not recognized as legitimate in the Roman world. For the next two and one-half centuries they, and all of Christianity, would live in the empire as an illegal and often persecuted religious sect.

But the deepest threat was internal. Everything about their faith had been cast in terms of faithful Jews who believed in Jesus the Messiah. Now that was challenged, torn away, lost! With pain and sorrow they must have asked, "How can we continue to believe in Jesus the Messiah if it divorces us from our roots, from the Judaism which we believe this faith fulfills?" Many must have been tempted to relinquish their faith in Jesus in order to retain their place in the Jewish community, exactly the intention of banishment. How could Christian leaders counsel their people not to give in, to keep the faith in spite of separation from family, friends and community? These must have been times of severe strain in the Johannine community.

The Signs Gospel, and the faith it presupposed, supplied them with no answers. The tacit assumption of a wonder-working Jewish messiah, upon which it was firmly based, was broken. What sense did it make to proclaim to Jews now that Jesus was the Messiah/prophet like Moses, if acceptance of that faith resulted in expulsion from the synagogue? Something more than the Signs Gospel's understated simplicity and Messianic faith was needed in this new situation.

Moreover, thrust out of the Jewish milieu into a more complex Roman environment, the miracle-worker message lost its effectiveness. The Hellenistic world was filled with the tales of wonder workers, of "god-men," *theioi andres*, who practiced the art of miraculous healing, predicting the future, levitation, etc. Virtually every Hellenistic city had a shrine dedicated to Aesculapius, the donkey-headed/human-bodied god of healing. Stories of the miraculous healings affected by this cult were commonplace. Even some of the Pharisaic rabbis, most notably Johanan ben Zakkai, had reputations as healers. So now the Johannine community, which had been nurtured on a Signs Gospel faith, found itself in a deep quandary. Their primary assumptions, the uniqueness of Jesus' mighty deeds and their proof he was the awaited Messiah, were rendered useless. Ironically, acceptance of the faith on its Jewish premises would result in expulsion from Judaism. In the Roman world, the claims for its wonder-working messiah were not particularly remarkable. If the community was going to survive in this new day, the message of the faith had to be rethought and restated.

That was the task the Fourth Evangelist set for himself. His revision of the Signs Gospel is so sweeping and so powerful that it easily overshadows the source upon which it is based. The revision was so thorough and so effective that a new tone, a new stress and new character were given to the Gospel. However, before examining the revision, it is important to ask, "Why did John revise the Signs Gospel?" If the most basic message of the Signs Gospel was in jeopardy, why not discard it and begin with something entirely new? The answer must lie in the importance that the community attached to the tradition represented by the Signs Gospel. Compare modern resistance to changes in hymns or Bible translations. By A.D. 85 the Johannine community had read, recited and revered the Signs Gospel for forty years. It was their foundation document, their charter of faith. It was as deeply entrenched in their understanding of the faith as are any traditional creeds, hymns or prayers in churches today.

Because of the esteem in which the Signs Gospel was held by the community, the way forward lay not in refuting or discarding the Signs Gospel, but in adapting it to this new and perilous time. In other words, for both John and his intended readers, the Signs Gospel was a natural, given starting point. And though finally the new Johannine faith of the revised Gospel may almost completely supersede the Signs Gospel faith, both John and his readers must have felt that it was a natural development of the tradition, not a repudiation. Otherwise the Gospel would not be written as it is nor would it have been accepted, honored and ultimately included in the New Testament.

The Prologue as Starting Point

The revision of the cherished Signs Gospel required a bold, positive approach. The hymn/poem we call the prologue provides just that fresh, striking beginning. It is uncertain whether the Evangelist began his work by choosing the prologue or, having completed the revision, he then realized how well the poem introduced his work. A majority of critics believe that the use of the prologue was the Evangelist's intention from the start.

The eighteen introductory verses provide clues to the source which the Evangelist used, and to his deliberate adaptation of it to serve his purpose. For decades now scholars have realized that a poem lies behind at least verses 1-13. Its nature can be seen in the opening stanza:

$$\overset{A}{\text{In}} \text{ beginning was the } \overset{B}{\text{Word}}$$

$$\text{And the } \overset{B}{\text{word}} \text{ was with [literally, to] } \overset{C}{\text{God}}$$

$$\text{And } \overset{C}{\text{God}} \text{ was the } \overset{B}{\text{Word}}$$

$$\overset{B}{\text{He}} \text{ was in } \overset{A}{\text{beginning}} \text{ with [to] } \overset{C}{\text{God}}.$$

(a very literal translation from the Greek)

In this rendering of the opening verses into English the super-scripted letters reveal the poetic pattern. The scheme is not that of rhyme and perhaps not even of meter (although a Hebrew or Aramaic original probably would have been metric), but that of a special sequence of repetition. The predicate of each line becomes the subject of the next line, so that it reads A-B, B-C, C-B, B-A, and thus a full circle is achieved. Except for the prose interruption of verses 6-8, a steady poetic rhythm based on repetition flows through the piece. A technical analysis is not necessary here to realize that a hymn/poem was adapted by the Evangelist to begin the new version of the Gospel.

Before exploring why the poem served the author so well, note should be made of his deliberate adaptations. Two of them are obvious. A reader quickly notes that verses 6-8 are in simple declarative prose that interrupts the flow of the poem. Most modern versions and translations also provide parentheses around verse 15 (Greek manuscripts are unpunctuated) because it, too, is a blatant prose interruption of its context. Both of these insertions point out, in sharp terms, that no one should make the mistake of thinking that John the Baptist is the subject of the hymn. The Baptist "was not the light," but "bore witness to him." The only plausible explanation for these sharp interruptions is that a continued rivalry with the followers of John the Baptist still existed for the Johannine community, and on that subject the author of the Signs Gospel and John were in full agreement. For both of them, John is subordinate to Jesus and overshadowed by him.

More telling is the way in which the Evangelist makes the hymn Christological. Even though some of the hymnic character is retained in the closing stanza (vs. 14, 16-18), it moves to a less cryptic and more direct affirmation of Christ, especially in verses 17-18. Not all critics agree, but most would hold that John added this stanza to the hymn to give it the climax that he wanted. It leaves the reader in no doubt as to the identity of the Word-Light-Life of the hymn. Modern readers, so familiar with the passage as to make it second nature, may be surprised to realize that Jesus is not even mentioned until late in verse 17. But the careful reader also senses a subtle but important shift in the prologue's view of Jesus away from that of the Signs Gospel. There, the signs validated Jesus. Here, the deeds

37

are not mentioned and the focus is on the person, presence, and function of Jesus. That is a vital clue to the Johannine message and to the revision of the Sign's Gospel theology.

No portion of the Bible has been so laboriously examined as the opening eighteen verses of John. A multitude of proposed models for the hymn source exist and as many proposals for the thought world from which it came. Suggestions have been made that the hymn was one already used by the Baptists about John (hence the careful denial of application to John), that it has been taken over from a Hellenistic/Gnostic tradition, that it was an existing Jewish hymn and that it was a hymn already applied to Jesus in the Johannine community. Definitive proof is not available, but recent studies have shown that the concepts of the hymn, especially the opening stanzas, are best paralleled in Jewish literature about wisdom. In that literature—Proverbs, Wisdom of Solomon and Odes of Solomon—wisdom is personified and almost divinized. Wisdom, too, is referred to as God's agent at creation, as the source of life and as dwelling or tabernacling with men (cf. 1:14 "dwelt" or "tabernacled"). So the strongest evidence about the background of the hymn seems to be the realm of Jewish speculation about wisdom.

That raises an immediate problem. The prologue is not about wisdom and never mentions it. Instead, the prologue speaks of "the Word" (Greek *logos*) which ultimately became flesh in Jesus. If the poem was about wisdom, why does John use Word in its place? The answer to that probably lies in the fact that wisdom is a feminine word both in Greek (*sophia*) and in Hebrew (*chokma*). To have used the term wisdom in writing the prologue would have caused an embarrassing change of gender in verse 17 when the subject of the hymn is personified in Jesus. Rather than do so, the Evangelist chose Word, which was masculine, and which also has a rich legacy in Jewish thought (the active word of Yahweh, *dawar*) as an agent of God's activity.

Whatever its source, the prologue deserves our close scrutiny for the bold purpose it serves for the Evangelist. The poetic form makes the passage striking to the eye and ear, even in the English translation. The major themes of the character of Jesus the Messiah are struck here for John in an exalted way. He is with God. He overcomes the darkness. He is the light, the life. In him we see grace and truth and glory, and we receive the power to become children of God. Even the dark tone of opposition is struck in verse 10 where the world is ignorant of him and in verse 11 where "his own people" do not receive him. Threads from these major themes reach forward to passage after passage and permeate the pages that follow. In that way, whether it was discovered by the Evangelist as an afterthought or was intended as an introduction by forethought, the prologue is a dramatic and powerful introduction to the current Gospel.

The closing stanza is the most crucial for the Evangelist. Here he is able at the outset to point the reader to the revelation of God's glory in Jesus. Glory will be an important theme throughout the Gospel. It was one of the strongest signs of God's presence in the Old Testament. The exultant words of Jesus at the supper scene (13:31), "Now is the Son of man glorified, and in him God is glorified," are but one example of this recurrent motif in the Gospel. Further, the emphasis on the uniqueness of Jesus, even over against Moses, is powerfully stated here. Moses gives only law; Jesus Christ brings grace and truth. Even more, Jesus is the only one who reveals the unseen God. "No one has ever seen God; the only Son, who is in the bosom of the Father, he has made him known" (1:18).

John's revision begins with this powerful introduction. No halfhearted revision of the Signs Gospel could hope to prove compelling to readers who cherished it *as it was*. But by opening with so beautiful and so forceful a poem, the writer could hope to capture and hold their attention. He could also propose a new way of seeing Jesus, a bold new vision that would compel the reader to read on to see how such a sweeping assertion could be maintained. From the start, the Evangelist chooses to confront the community's key problem directly. A simple faith in a wonder-working Jesus had lost its power. In the bold strokes of the prologue, John proposes a much more inclusive Christology with Jesus as Word, Life, Light, bringer of glory, grace and truth; as not only Messiah but as God's Son.

One further word about the prologue is necessary. The choice of "the Word" rather than wisdom solved one problem and created another. Later Gentile Christian readers of the Gospel, as early as Irenaeus (c. A.D. 175), saw *logos* and immediately thought of the term's use in Greek philosophy from Plato to their Stoic contemporaries, where it meant the rational principle of the universe. Such readers then saw in John a Greek philosophical approach to the Christian faith. Nearly nineteen hundred years of interpretation of the Gospel have been distorted by that approach. Aside from the fact that the actual subject matter of the Gospel certainly is not Greek philosophical discussion, these interpreters (even many today) have failed to note that the Word is the only theme word from the prologue that does not recur in the rest of the Gospel. That alone suggests that it is a mistake to think of John as the "Gospel for the Greek," as has been said so often. Apparently the concept of the Word held no further interest for the Evangelist. Perhaps, too, that is final and conclusive proof that a hymn source lies behind the prologue, a hymn source whose key word was useful to the author only at 1:14, "the Word became flesh and dwelt among us," and afterward received no attention. The Signs Gospel probably began as a narrative with verse 19. It was a bold stroke of a great thinker to introduce a revision of the Signs Gospel by the powerful poetry of the prologue compelling his audience to read on.

Suggested Supplementary Reading

R. E. Brown, *Anchor Bible*, Vol. 29, gives an extensive treatment of research on the prologue, including alternative reconstructions to the one he prefers.

Questions and Suggestions for Study

1. Choose one or two key words in the prologue and look them up in a concordance. How frequent and widespread is their use in the rest of the Gospel? Does this correlate with the hymn-source theory?

2. Write out the prologue in a more stanza-like fashion (omitting vs. 6-8 and v. 15). What elements of poetic character emerge?

The Signs Become Dramas of Contemporary Faith

With the prologue as a poetic and Christological starting point, the Evangelist was able to redirect the use and meaning of the signs. Where the signs had been miracle stories directly and briefly told, several of them now became the starting point for extended dramas and dialogues about the meaning of Christian faith. The most obvious instance and the one easiest to follow is the expansion of the story in 9:1-7 of the man born blind:

> As he passed by, he saw a man blind from his birth. And his disciples asked him, "Rabbi, who sinned, this man or his parents, that he was born blind?" Jesus answered, "It was not

that this man sinned, or his parents, but that the works of God might be made manifest in him. We must work the works of him who sent me, while it is day; night comes, when no one can work. As long as I am in the world, I am the light of the world." As he said this, he spat on the ground and made clay of the spittle and anointed the man's eyes with the clay, saying to him, "Go, wash in the pool of Siloam" (which means Sent). So he went and washed and came back seeing.

It is quite likely that the Signs Gospel version of the miracle consisted simply of verses 1-3, with a location given in the setting, and of verses 6-7. There would also have been a statement like that which concludes the healing of the official's son in 4:53, "And he himself believed, and all his household," followed by a conclusion giving the number of the sign (e.g. "This was the fourth sign which Jesus did . . ."). The Evangelist expanded the story in a sequence of dramatic scenes. The expansion now becomes the center of the reader's attention because the subsequent fate of the healed one looms larger than the healing itself.

The only changes that the author made within the recital of the sign are the explanation of the works of God in verses 4-5 and the translation of Siloam in verse 7. That the first explanation is an insertion is apparent in the shift of pronouns from third person to first person. (The shift in verse 4 from "we" to "me" can be explained better later in this study.) The presence of these favorite Johannine themes—"him who sent me," "night comes," and "I am the light of the world"—also point clearly to the Evangelist's hand.

But the thirty-three-verse expansion of the miracle is the major work of the Evangelist here. In a series of carefully drawn scenes, he portrays the aftermath of the blind man's healing. The scenes may be outlined as follows:

    I. The blind man and the neighbors discuss the event (vs. 8-12).

    II. The Pharisees interrogate the blind man (vs. 13-17).

    III. The Pharisees interrogate the blind man's parents (vs. 18-23).

IV. The Pharisees interrogate the blind man a second time and finally cast him out (vs. 24-34).
V. The blind man encounters Jesus again and comes to believe (vs. 35-38).
VI. Jesus and the Pharisees exchange bitter words (vs. 39-41).

If there is any doubt that this dramatic expansion is the work of the Evangelist, it is quickly dispelled by verses 22 and 34. Both verses are direct references to expulsion from the synagogue for belief in Jesus. Chapter 9 can come only from a writer in a situation where the Jews had already agreed to put believers in Jesus out of the synagogue. Since the Pharisees had no such control over Judaism before A.D. 70, the context of the dramatic expansion in chapter 9 must be the life of the church in John's own day. In John's world, a synagogue Jew under suspicion of the Christian heresy could be called in by the synagogue council, as could the family, and anyone convicted could be expelled. This was a fact of life for John's church. It had happened to some, if not many, of its members.

Two features of this dramatic expansion are critical to understanding John. First, he told a story that is unmistakably set in the time when Jesus was alive in his ministry and then attached to it a drama that is just as unmistakably set in John's own day and time, fifty years later. In other words, John freely superimposed his own day's story upon the Jesus story from the Signs Gospel, which, authentic or not, he and his readers believed had happened in Jesus' time. By doing this, John puts words and events from his time into the mouth and life of Jesus. How could he have the nerve to do such a thing? How could the readers tolerate it? Answers to those questions are imbedded in a major difference between early Christianity and the modern world.

The current generation are children of a critical time, not at all comfortable with letting anyone but Jesus, Plato, or any other ancient figure speak for themselves. But the early Christians did not live with a sense of separation between the past life of Jesus and their present life. For them the present was lived in community headed by the risen Lord, the same Lord who had taught and healed in Galilee. Evidence of this is shown in Paul's letters and in Acts where the contemporary words of Christian prophets announcing "Thus says the Lord," by the power of the Spirit, were taken to be just as much words of Jesus as words that he spoke during the earthly ministry. Neither John nor his readers have the least qualm about merging the past of Jesus' day and the now of their day into a single story. The issue for them is the validity of the Gospel message for their day, not the discordant time frames. Once this fact is grasped, the power of the message to John's troubled readers and his genius are glimpsed in the writing. In his hands, a gospel message which was outdated and even troubling became once again a word of life and faith for them in their own day.

Much can also be learned in the way the story is actually developed in the course of the dramatic expansion. The Signs Gospel author had stressed that all one needed for faith was the simple evidence of the mighty wonders of Jesus. Applied to this case that would mean that the blind man, and probably his family, would rejoice in the healing and immediately believe in Jesus because of the sign. But in the Evangelist's new story this is not what happens at all. Instead, the parents never do come to faith because they fear expulsion from the synagogue. And the blind man does not come to faith until *after* he has been expelled from the synagogue. Even then he does so not because of the healing, but as a result of a further encounter and dialogue with Jesus.

But how could someone who had been expelled from the synagogue encounter Jesus and be led to faith? Jesus was no longer around! Once again our perspective blocks an appreciation of the point of view of the early church. For them Jesus was still present in the living community and its representatives. This story not only says to readers that expulsion from the synagogue is not an end but a beginning, but it also reinforces their belief in the righteousness of their continuing to be faithful *in spite of* expulsion. In receiving those who are expelled from the synagogue, the church continues the ministry of Jesus to which it is called. Thus, "*we* must work the works of him who sent *me*," now has much more meaning that it originally did as we read the sign.

Further, the basis for Christian faith is no longer to be found simply in accepting the proof of the miracles of Jesus the Messiah/prophet like Moses. The sign has not been denied or refuted, but in John's new Gospel it does not cause or prompt faith. Faith occurs in a personal encounter and decision on the part of the healed man. Thus, without rejecting the Signs Gospel outright, John has so restated that faith that the basis now is a different Christology: Son of man replaces Messiah in the faith encounter (9:35), and it is also a different experience. Both of these are more fitting for the faith problems of John's day and time.

John 9 is not an isolated instance. Chapters 5 and 7 exhibit a similar expansion of the story of the healing of the paralytic at the pool of Bethzatha. There, too, the signs story leads to a controversy between the healed person and the Jews. The story develops into a confrontation between Jesus and his opponents, a controversy filled with foreboding because the opponents seek to kill Jesus (5:18; 7:1, 19, 25, etc.). But in that story the healed man drops out of sight and never comes to faith. The sign in those chapters is not a vehicle to faith but an object upon which the opponents seize to center their hostility. Yet, so vivid is the expanded dialogue that the reader hardly notices that the original sign has entirely lost its original function. In a similar, but less formally exact way, the story of the raising of Lazarus has been expanded in chapter 11 to become another reinterpreted sign. There, however, much of the dramatic expansion occurs within the story itself and the shape of the original sign is virtually lost. That story, too, ends with an ominous discussion among the Jewish opponents about the necessity for the execution of Jesus.

One of the most prevalent and effective ways in which John revised the Signs Gospel was by *expanding* the already existing signs. In so doing, he sought to transform the original miracle stories into stories of the significance of faith in Jesus in his day. John invited his Christian readers, who were feeling alienated after expulsion from the synagogue, to journey on in the continuing story of Jesus on a new plane that made sense of the dilemmas of their lives.

Suggested Supplementary Reading

The reader who wishes to pursue the topic of the dramatic expansions in John and their significance should read J. L. Martyn, *History and Theology in the Fourth Gospel.*

Questions and Suggestions for Study

1. Mark off the miracle in John 5 from its expansion. Do you agree that chapter 7 picks up from chapter 5? If so, why is chapter 6 where it is? (That puzzle, recognized for centuries, remains unsolved but will be discussed in the next section.)

2. Martyn argues that the threats to kill Jesus reflect actual threats to kill Christian leaders in John's day, so that they had to avoid the Jewish quarter of their town(s). Do you see any evidence for this?

3. Notice how skillfully the Evangelist connected the expansion in chapter 9 back to the original sign in verse 34. What is the clue?

6

A Sign Leads to a Sermon

Just as John was able to give meaning to his faith by expanding the sign in John 9, or in chapter 5, to a drama of encounter, he was also able to use in a special way the signs source in chapter 6 as a springboard for an address by Jesus. That address is unique and teaches a great deal about the Evangelist's thought.

The placement of chapter 6 is one of the enduring puzzles of the Fourth Gospel. It begins, "After this Jesus went to the other side of the Sea of Galilee," but he isn't in Galilee. Chapter 5 is set in Jerusalem. And chapter 6 seems to interrupt the dialogue which began in chapter 5 and is resumed, though awkwardly, in 7:1-10. While some have argued that the pages of John must have been shuffled very early and that chapter 6 belongs ahead of chapter 5, that does nothing to explain the awkward transition in chapter 7. So it seems probable that the Evangelist, working as he was from the Signs Gospel, cared little for precise transitions of geography and arranged the Gospel this way himself. In any case, chapter 6 comprises a special unit for our consideration.

The chapter begins with the stories of the feeding of the five thousand and of Jesus walking on the water (vs. 1-21), in the same sequence as found in Mark 6 and Matthew 14. But John carries on the issue by having a crowd seek out Jesus so that a debate ensues about the meaning of the feeding miracle. Why this order? Why, if the issue is the feeding miracle, is the story of the walking on the water allowed to interrupt? There are two good reasons for that. First, that is how the miracles stood in the Signs Gospel. That the feeding miracle is from that source is confirmed by verse 14, "When the people saw the sign which he had done, they said, 'This is indeed the prophet who is to come into the world!'" This comment, absent from Matthew and Mark, stresses both the sign and the prophetic expectation of the Signs Gospel. The second reason the stories are together is that the two miracles were probably linked in the oral tradition before the writing of the Signs Gospel, Mark, or Matthew. Because of that John does not think of separating them, or of eliminating the second miracle; he simply turns his attention to the sign which interests him.

The dialogue which follows, though dominated by the comments of Jesus, is interspersed with comments, criticisms and suggestions from the Jews. Since Jesus was a Jew, the first disciples were Jews, and in all likelihood John and most of his readers were Jews, it is puzzling that the opponents of Jesus could simply be named "the Jews." That problem may be made clearer when it is realized that the author of the Gospel of Matthew, in spite of his intense hostility to Pharisaism, never speaks of the Jews as opposed to Jesus. How can John?

A glance back to the drama just discussed may help answer this question. There it is the Pharisees who investigate the

incident of the healing of the blind man (John 9:13, 24, 40).
But the author can use "the Jews" as a synonym for the Pharisees in that story in three cases (vs. 18, 22). That must mean
that the separation of church and synagogue had gone so far
that the expelled Christians, Jews by birth, no longer identified
themselves with Judaism and identified Pharisees and Judaism
as one phenomenon. In other words, for John and his readers,
"the Jews" was not an ethnic or racial term but a religious term
reserved for the dominant Pharisaic synagogue community.
Christians today need to be precise about this distinction
because of the ugly reality of anti-Semitism. The division in
John's time is a *religious* split between people of the *same*
ethnic origin. It should not be termed, or used to support,
anti-Semitic bigotry.

A brief controversy with the Jews who are seeking Jesus
provides the backdrop for the Johannine sermon on the bread
of life. They ask, "When did you come here?" (6:25) because
they had not seen him leave the other side of the lake. Instead
of answering them, Jesus challenges their reason for looking
for him, saying that they only want more food. The reader will
note that the technique of the non-answer or unexpected
answer is a favorite of the Evangelist (cf. 3:3 and 4:10). It puts
Jesus, and not the questioners, in control of the dialogue.

This leads to the key challenge from the opponents, "What
sign do you do, that we may see, and believe you?" (v. 30).
(Remember that they had witnessed the feeding miracle.) "Our
fathers ate the manna in the wilderness; as it is written, 'He
gave them bread from heaven to eat'" (v. 31). The careful
construction was derived from the feeding sign and led to the
citation of a scripture text by the opponents. From that point
the Evangelist constructed a homily on that text.

The Synagogue Sermon Form

A number of recent studies have shown that by the first
century A.D. the technique of scripture interpretation in the
synagogue service had evolved into some set patterns. The
most popular one was probably the style now called key-word

or catch-word interpretation of the Torah text for that day. Such an interpretation had a well-defined form.

In the synagogue service the scripture would be read, a text from the Torah (Genesis-Deuteronomy), and then it would be translated into Aramaic (called a *Targum*) for the sake of those who did not know Hebrew. Then the speaker— an elder, rabbi or respected teacher—would provide a comment on the text. He would begin by telling the congregation how he was pronouncing the unpointed Hebrew. Since Hebrew is written only in consonants and the vowels are to be supplied, there is considerable leeway in terms of tenses, pronouns and plurals in the reading of the text. Ordinarily, the context gives the reader the intended meaning and the pronunciation follows. However, the tradition held that in giving the Torah to Moses, God intended all the possible meanings of the written text. It was a technique that allowed the Torah to be much more widely applied to the issues of the present day. Paul, a former Pharisee, is doing exactly this in Galatians 3:16 when he reads *offspring* (singular) instead of *offsprings* (plural) in Genesis 12:7.

Once the speaker had established the reading of the text, the homily proceeded in a set fashion. The speaker chose three or four key words from the text and commented on them, one by one. In the course of these comments it was expected that he would make reference to a secondary Old Testament scripture, from the Prophets or the Writings, as a way of showing the essential unity of God's revelation. Finally, when all the key words had received comment, the homily would conclude with a paraphrase of the original text in light of the explanation the speaker had given. We find examples of this sermonic technique in the oldest Rabbinic Midrashim (commentaries), in the work of the Hellenistic Jewish writer Philo of Alexandria (c. A.D. 40-70) and in the letters of Paul.

The Johannine Sermon on the Bread of Life

By expanding the Signs Gospel miracle into a dialogue, John has made the feeding miracle the occasion for a debate

---

The Sign and the Sermon of John 6*

I. The feeding of the 5,000 and the walking on the water, 6:1-21 (A "Sign" from the Signs Gospel).

II. The Jewish opponents introduce the Torah text, 6:31, "He gave them bread from heaven to eat."

III. Jesus establishes the "reading" of the text, 6:32b, "My Father gives you the true bread from heaven."

IV. The Interpretation of the text, 6:35-57.

    A. Comment on *the bread*, 6:35-40.
    B. Comment on *from heaven*, 6:41-47.
    C. Comment on *to eat*, 6:48-57.
    D. The supporting text from the prophets, 6:45.

V. The Recapitulation of the Sermon, 6:58, "This is the bread which came down from heaven."

---

about Moses and Jesus that centers on the issue of the miracle of the manna in the wilderness. It may well be that the Signs Gospel community had used the feeding miracle to show that Jesus was like Moses in miraculously providing bread. If so, John's treatment is not directed at Jewish opponents but at a Christian misunderstanding of the sign because he does not give that expected reply.

The challenge, "What sign do *you* do? Our fathers ate manna in the wilderness. He [Moses] gave them bread from heaven to eat," utilizes a combined text from Exodus (16:4, 15), which was a common way of dealing with Old Testament stories in sermon and commentary. To that Jesus replies, "It was not Moses who gave you the bread from heaven; my Father gives you the true bread from heaven" (John 6:32). Here is the corrected reading of the text. "He" of the text is to

---

*Based on P. Borgen, *Bread from Heaven*, pp. 28-51.

be understood as my "Father," and not as Moses. The verb is to be read as present tense "gives" and not the past tense "gave." And the indirect object is to be read as "you" or "to you" instead of "them." Thus, the corrected reading of the Exodus text for the purposes of this discussion is to be, "My Father gives you the true bread from heaven to eat."

In the verses that follow, the Johannine Jesus comments on the key words of that text. In verses 35-40 comes the ringing affirmation, "I am the bread of life." Then in verses 43-51 there is a comment on the meaning of "from heaven" as "I am the living bread which comes down from heaven." In that second paragraph of the homily, the secondary text from Isaiah 54:13 is introduced: "It is written in the prophets, 'And they shall all be taught by God'" (v. 45). Finally, in verses 52-57, there is an extended comment on the significance of the verb "to eat" by application to the Lord's Supper: "Truly truly, I say to you, unless you eat the flesh of the Son of Man and drink his blood, you have no life in you." The conclusion of the homily is reached in verse 58 when the original text is restated in a paraphrase, "This is the bread which came down from heaven, that a man may eat of it and not die."

The discovery of this homily in John 6 was made by Peder Borgen in *Bread from Heaven* and it helps explain several puzzling things about this chapter. The first, and simplest, is a case of mistranslation in most versions of the chapter. John 6:36 in the Revised Standard Version reads, "But I said to you that you have seen me and yet do not believe." That is one grammatically correct way of reading the verse in Greek, but it does not make sense in the context. Jesus has not said, anywhere, "You have seen me and yet do not believe." However, in recalling that the Evangelist made a point of reading "my Father gives *you*" instead of "he gave *them*" a quite different reading emerges. The word which the Revised Standard Version translates "that" (in Greek *oti*) can either introduce indirect address, as the Revised Standard Version reads it, or it can mean "because." The Johannine passage makes far better sense if 6:36 is read this way: "But I said, *you*, because you have seen me and yet do not believe." It further illustrates how precisely the Evangelist has constructed the homily in this chapter.

The other problems which John 6 presents are far more substantial. John 9 shows that the Evangelist has no qualms about telescoping the time of Jesus and the time of his own day into one dramatic story. In so doing, the readers of John's own day gain an insight about the meaning of their present difficulties. That was John's purpose. But he also describes scenes in which Jesus participates that *could not actually have happened.* No one was cast out of the synagogue for belief in Jesus *before* Jesus died. The expansion of the story of the blind man to include events more than a generation later troubles historically oriented minds and forces today's readers either to see John as falsifying the story, or to believe the impossible event in order to protect the integrity of the Gospel. Once again, this trap is broken out of by realizing that John and his readers did not share our attitudes toward the Jesus story. For them the Jesus of history, and the Jesus who was present as Lord of their community, was one Jesus and his story was one story. Today's readers cannot go back to that way of thinking, perhaps, but can understand that neither John nor his readers thought he was falsifying the Jesus story by applying it directly to his own day and time.

That perspective is vital to all Gospel studies, but is especially important when dealing with John 6. The words of Jesus in this chapter are not words that Jesus of Nazareth ever spoke in Palestine during his ministry. They are the creative vision of the Evangelist as he gave meaning to the sign of the feeding of the five thousand. There seems to be no reminiscence of Jesus' actual words here, although some scholars, including R.E. Brown, debate that. The homily is too precise. The text and secondary text are too convenient. The discourse is tied up so carefully and the language is so thoroughly Johannine that John 6:25-29 must be assigned to the creative genius of John.

But if in recognizing this is sensed a loss of contact with what Jesus actually said, something is also gained. Granted, the discourses and dialogues in John are not memories of actual events in Jesus' time, but they do represent an early attempt by a great Christian thinker to recast the faith into a form that could deal with the issues, the problems and the anxieties of the new situation in post-war Palestine/Syria. Since that is a task to which every generation is inevitably called, and since mere repetition of the past tradition never suffices, a grasp of one of the earliest attempts to restate the faith can both inform efforts and spur Christians today to the same task.

When the Gospel is viewed in that way, one can see what John was doing in the homily of John 6. He and his readers were as familiar with that form of address as modern Protestants are with sermons that have three points. It was a natural way of expression. The content is what counts. In the controversy with Pharisaic Judaism, Jesus and Moses were inevitably set in competition. As they interrogate the blind man in John 9:28, the Pharisees charge, "You are his disciple, but we are disciples of Moses." And in that confrontation John consistently says to his readers that Jesus completely transcends Moses. Through Moses manna was given in the wilderness, but Jesus himself is the Bread of Life. That is the drumbeat message of the homily. Remember that already in the prologue this theme had been struck, "for the law was given through Moses; grace and truth came through Jesus Christ" (v. 17). And the subtle critique of the Signs Gospel faith continues here. The feeding miracle does not produce faith; faith depends on a response to Jesus himself and *not* on his miracles. Not everyone will agree with this Johannine change, but the Evangelist is an outspoken apologist for a faith based on who Jesus is, not on what he did.

Those insights also help deal with the most difficult portion of this chapter, verses 51-58. If the living Jesus of Galilee had actually said to an audience, "He who eats my flesh and drinks my blood abides in me, and I in him" (v. 56), there would have been no possible meaning for the words other than a weird kind of cannibalism. No contemporary of Jesus could have known about the future Last Supper or of its subsequent use as the most sacred Christian ritual. But in the context of the church of John's day it makes sense. John makes participation in the Lord's Supper, the community's precious ceremony remembering and re-encountering Jesus, the key to the new identity of those who have been torn away from their Mosaic heritage. Some critics, recoiling at the crude expression in verses 51-58 of so blatant a sacramental under-standing of the Lord's Supper, want to assign this passage to a later editor.[2] However, Borgen appears to be correct in point-ing out that verses 51-58 are vital to the complete homily, that they share Johannine language and should not be assigned to another writer because they are troubling. For the Christians who were enduring expulsion from the synagogue, John's stir-ring redirection of the faith through a rewrite of the Signs Gospel, and through the familiar device of a homily on a Torah text, must have come as a fresh, new insight in troubled times.

Suggested Supplementary Reading

The classic study on John 6 is that of Peder Borgen, *Bread from Heaven* (Leiden: E.J. Brill, 1965).

See also R.E. Brown's discussion of John 6 in the *Anchor Bible*, Vol. 29, and his proposed translation of verse 36.

Questions and Suggestions for Study

1. Using different colored pencils underline separately all the instances in John 6:31-58 of 1) "bread," 2) "from heaven," and 3) "to eat." Note how interwoven these words from the Torah text are in the whole passage.

2. Discuss your reaction to the strong evidence that these words really come from John and not Jesus. What do you feel you lose? What do you gain?

Other Johannine Stresses

A number of dialogues and scenes of the Fourth Gospel, drawn from oral tradition as well as from the Signs Gospel, are used by the Evangelist as openings for his discussion of the new meaning of faith. Some of the most obvious ones are the encounter with Nicodemus in chapter 3 (perhaps in the same tradition as the Synoptics' "rich young man"), the discussion with the Samaritan woman at the well of Sychar in chapter 4, and the revision of the Lord's Supper tradition in chapter 13 (where no account of Jesus' words at the meal is given). All of these cases further illustrate that John is primarily interested in presenting the new version of faith through the vehicle of the Gospel and that, for him, the traditional incidents are secondary.

Several general features of the revision need to be emphasized. They recur in a number of Johannine passages. The first is a series of assertions that begin with, "I am . . . ." An encounter with two of these—"I am the light of the world" (9:5) and "I am the bread of life" (6:35ff)—occurred in early sections of this book. For many readers this is the single most striking difference between the portrayal of Jesus in the Fourth Gospel and that of the Synoptic gospels. In the other Gospels Jesus is presented as very reluctant to speak of his own identity. Especially in the oldest teaching traditions, the parables and the short sayings, any reference to Jesus himself can only be derived by inference. Jesus does not promote himself directly. Yet here in John, Jesus speaks directly about himself time and again and does so in sweepingly dramatic, almost arrogant, terms. It is important to account for this great difference in the early Christian portrayal of Jesus. He cannot have been as reluctant to speak of himself as the Synoptics say and, at the same time, as direct about his identity as the Fourth Gospel's Jesus is. Almost all critics today agree that there is no evidence that Jesus ever adopted any title for himself, except possibly the enigmatic title "Son of Man," and that the ascription of such titles to Jesus, even in the Gospels of Matthew, Mark and Luke, reflects the post-Easter faith of the early church, not the perspective of Jesus himself.

Therefore, when Jesus says in the Johannine discourses, "I am the light of the world" (8:12, 9:5), "I am the door of the sheep"(10:7), "I am the good shepherd" (10:11,14), "I am the resurrection and the life" (11:25), and the famous "I am the way, and the truth, and the life" (14:6), these are the faith affirmation of the Evangelist, not Jesus. He has put his theology into this dramatic, first-person Gospel form more than any other evangelist has. And, while the boldness and the exclusiveness of these ringing assertions about Jesus may trouble some, the purpose they served must be kept in mind.

John's Christian community had been stripped of its faith foundations by exclusion from the synagogue. Their anchors in the faith of Abraham, Moses and David had been deeply shaken. John's bold Christological assertions are meant to fill that gap and assure the Christian community that it remains, through its faith in the crucified and risen Jesus, firmly rooted in the eternal plan and purpose of God. These assertions echo the prologue's bold assertion that the revelation which the Christian community has encountered in Jesus is a genuine expression of the will and purpose of God.

Whether these assertions, simply taken over from the Evangelist, are valid for the life of Christian people today is a question to be discussed at the end of this study. Here, approval or disapproval must be left aside and an appreciation of what the Evangelist tried to accomplish must be developed. He turned his readers' attention from the issues of whether Jesus had been an exact fulfillment of Davidic and Mosaic hopes, to the question of how much Jesus was God's new revelation in his own right and without the need for external verification. That was the major accomplishment of John, and it helped the troubled Johannine community, and ultimately perhaps all of Christianity, to turn a faith corner. That is the function of the bold "I am . . ." in the Fourth Gospel.

An Altered View of Time

Another feature of the Evangelist's revised way of presenting the faith is the New Testament's most radical revision of the early Christian view of time and history. Earliest Christianity was thoroughly apocalyptic. The Christian community was not founded on a belief that Jesus had been or even is the Messiah, but on the firm hope that Jesus is the coming Messiah. They viewed the time after the resurrection as a brief interval before Jesus would return in triumph to judge the world. That view was shared by all the early Christians. Paul clearly expected to see the end as he wrote both in 1 Thessalonians (early) and 1 Corinthians (late): "Then we who are alive . . . shall be caught up together with them [the risen dead] in the clouds to meet the Lord in the air. . ." (1 Thessalonians 4:17) and "We shall not all sleep, but we shall all be changed" (1 Corinthians 15:51). No convincing evidence shows that

59

Paul ever changed that position. The Galileans who had abandoned homes and livelihoods to emigrate to Jerusalem and live from a shared purse could only have done so in the belief that time was very short (Acts 2:43-47). Both Mark and Matthew exhort their readers to a renewed faith in the imminent end of the age. The Book of Revelation is devoted to this theme. Even the author of Luke-Acts, who feels the strain of time passing and the end not yet come, only postpones the end to an indefinite future for which the church should always be ready. Early Christianity was firmly set in a belief that the end of the present age was near and that Christ's return and the judgment would draw down the curtain of history and inaugurate the longed-for kingdom of heaven.

The Signs Gospel faith must have stood within that apocalyptic framework as well. The crucified/risen Jesus was presented as the promised Messiah/prophet like Moses on the same premise that faith in him was imperative for the imminent end of the age. But more than fifty some years had passed and the glowing expectation of an earlier day had grown thin for the Christians of John's day.

The Evangelist's solution to this problem is a striking one. In view of the futuristic, apocalyptic bent of so much early Christianity, his stress on present fulfillment stands out boldly. Ever since the work of Rudolf Bultmann, some have argued that John completely disavowed apocalyptic belief in favor of present salvation that simply continues on beyond death, as in the Greek and modern belief in immortality. Several passages in John do read best in that fashion: "If anyone eats of this bread, he will live forever"(6:51); "That whoever believes in him should not perish but have eternal life" (3:16); "And I give them eternal life, and they shall never perish" (10:28); and, "Whoever lives and believes in me shall never die"(11:26).

But other passages, in the same contexts, suggest a belief in both present and future hope *without* denying death and future resurrection. For example, "He who eats my flesh and drinks my blood has eternal life, and I will raise him up at the last day" (6:54), and "He who believes in me, though he die, yet shall he live" (11:25). It is doubtful that all of these futuristic sayings were cleverly added by a later editor. They pointed to a Johannine view that real life, eternal life, begins *now* with faith in Jesus and will continue, or be resumed, at the last day. But the focus in this Gospel is on the *now* of salvation. For the Evangelist, now is the time of salvation: "The hour is coming, and now is, when the true worshipers will worship the Father in spirit and truth" (4:23). John firmly believes that faith in Jesus leads to new life *now* because it has been brought by Jesus himself. There is nothing more to wait for. So, even if he retained the rudiments of a futuristic hope, the Evangelist made the boldest shift of the New Testament to a full and present reality of the life promised by God and brought in Jesus.

The Ethic for a New Day

Another theme of the Johannine discourses also deserves attention and needs to be discussed as the contemporary value of the Gospel is assessed. A wealth of material in Matthew, Mark, and Luke is devoted to ethical teaching and is familiar to Christians today. The Sermon on the Mount/Sermon on the Plain tradition clearly points out the ethical focus from and about Jesus in the early church. In the Fourth Gospel, this focus is missing almost entirely. There are no debates or sayings about such issues as divorce, keeping the Torah, Sabbath observance or love of enemies. There are no instructions about how to act in the dawning reign of God. The Gospel of John has little to say, in any of its stages, about the ethical and moral issues of Christian life.

So what the Gospel does say about action in John 13 and 14 deserves careful attention. These Johannine emphases give some idea of the Evangelist's outlook. First, he implies at several points that his readers already know the ethical tradition from Jesus ("my commandments") so well that they do not need to be spelled out: "He who has my commandments and keeps them, he it is who loves me" (14:21); "If you love me, you will keep my commandments" (14:15); "If anyone hears my sayings and does not keep them, I do not judge him" (12:47). These and other verses leave little doubt that the Johannine community knew of a basic commandments tradition from Jesus which it presupposed. It is also clear that the spelling out of that tradition was not part of the Evangelist's purpose. That does not mean that the Evangelist and his community were unethical. It means only that the author chose not to stress that feature of the Gospel.

But he does stress one aspect of the commandments of Jesus. Indeed, it may be that John creates a commandment:

> A new commandment I give to you, that you love one another; even as I have loved you, that you also love one another. By this all men will know that you are my disciples, if you have love for one another (13:34-35).

The stress on this new commandment occurs at the Last Supper scene. It is reinforced by John's special version of that scene, for the washing of the disciples' feet by Jesus is an acted-out example of Jesus' care for them. It is explained to them in exactly that way: "For I have given you an example, that you also should do as I have done to you. Truly, truly, I say to you, a servant is not greater than his master" (13:15-16).

Nowhere else in the gospel tradition is there so strong an emphasis on Christian love of one another. This theme became a dominant one in the Johannine community, where the Gospel was once more revised and the Johannine epistles were written. In Matthew the saying "a servant is not above his master" (10:24) is a counsel to humility. In John it is *both* a call to humility and a concrete example of how Christians should love one another. Only in the very similar exhortations to communal care and concern in Paul's letters is there found a parallel New Testament emphasis on the love of Christians for one another (1 Corinthians 12 and 13, Philippians 2:5-12, etc.).

That parallel with Paul helps us to understand John. Paul was writing to newly formed, isolated, fledgling churches that needed to survive as communities. Competition, factiousness and jealousy were real threats to their existence, as the Corinthian correspondence makes clear. So, too, John was writing for a Christian community in crisis. It had been cut off from its Jewish home base and now had to survive on its own in an alien world. In this new day, the nurturing love within the community was needed *above all else*. So the Evangelist, while assuming the rest of the Christian ethical tradition, felt a need to stress the new commandment to love one another. It was a vital necessity for these beleaguered Christians. It meant life or death to their communities and it would mark them as Jesus' disciples in a positive way in a hostile world.

Too often this aspect of the early Christian faith is forgotten in modern, Western discussion of the faith in our stress on theology, history and credo. Social justice, love even of the enemy, and an outgoing love for the world are major hallmarks of the Christian heritage. But it was also true, and may still be true, that the Christian communities were able to endure centuries of persecuted existence because of their radical commitment to one another. Early in the second century the Roman governor of Egypt wrote to the emperor about the Christian community, "See how they love one another." It was the communal concern of Christians that allowed them to weather those storms. Under the pressure of his new day, John understood that love for one another was vital to the faith and life of his readers.

Suggested Supplementary Reading
On the "I am" speeches and the realized eschatology of the Fourth Gospel, a good further resource is R. Kysar's study book, *John, the Maverick Gospel.*

Questions and Suggestions for Study

1. Because he changed the focus of the view of the end of the world and the meaning of salvation, John is often treated as a "mystical" Gospel. Mysticism means individual, personal oneness with the divine. Is it accurate to speak of the Johannine faith in this way? Why or why not?

2. Use a concordance to locate all the "I am" sayings in John. Note that they are all in the Evangelist's revision and not part of the original signs stories. Do you agree with the statement that these are the Evangelist's faith affirmations? Why or why not?

3. In what ways is the Johannine emphasis on "love one another" good? What are its dangers?

8

"The One Sent from God"— The Johannine Model for Jesus

As has been illustrated in a number of ways, the special genius of the Christian writer who revised the Signs Gospel was a gift for taking the old tradition and reusing it in a way which breathed new life and faith for the day in which he lived. Even if some of John's adaptations prove to be outworn and useless for modern times, just like the Signs Gospel was in his time, John showed early in the Christian story that the Gospel must be continually rethought and renewed in terms appropriate to new times and situations. This chapter deals with the most important adaptation John made.

A preliminary word is necessary about the role of analogy and model in religious thought. Old Testament scholars have known for a long time that the creation story in Genesis 1 is modeled on Babylonian ideas of the world's being formed out of a watery chaos. Its verses paint a picture of God's creating in that way. It is not a scientific picture but a poetic, mythical picture. Its point is that God is the source of existence and that the world given to human beings is good. Jesus used the analogy of "Father" to help his disciples, and himself, envision God. That does not mean that God is a male human person with sex organs, beard, etc. It means that the human image of a loving parent helps us relate to the power beyond the reach of our ordinary experience. Paul's letters are filled with analogies—of courtroom acquittal, of Roman legal adoption, of the church as the human body, or the resurrection as comparable to seeds or stars. Except for the capacity to say what the ultimate is not *(via negativa)*, human minds are bound to the need for analogy to express precious concerns. John is no exception.

The feature of John's revision that has been most overlooked by the great surge of recent scholarship has been the fundamental model by which he envisioned Jesus. One way of getting near it is by observing John's language. While the favorite Johannine titles for Jesus, "Son of God" and "Son of man," occur only thirteen and ten times in the Gospel, respectively, Jesus is described as "sent by God" fifty-nine times. A reader who underlines those uses will quickly see that it is a term that almost always occurs in John's work, not in the Signs Gospel stories. So from the point of view of language, John stressed in an unprecedented way the idea that Jesus is sent from God. This is a general idea, not a technical term, because John freely mixes the two synonymous Greek words for "send" throughout the Gospel. These words are *apostello*, which is the root word of apostle, and *pempo*.

The most striking evidence of John's use of "sent" is in three places where the Evangelist gives an editorial aside:

1. "We must work the works of him who sent me" (9:4).

2. "I knew that thou hearest me always, but I have said this on account of the people standing by, that they may believe that thou didst send me" (11:42).

3. "And this is eternal life, that they know thee the only true God, and Jesus Christ whom thou hast sent" (17:3). John's view of Jesus was dominated by the idea that Jesus was sent by God. What did the Evangelist mean by it?

Although there has been some debate about the background of the idea of the sent one, especially from those who believe that the New Testament was deeply influenced by developing Gnostic thought, it seems clear that the sending concept is rooted in one of the oldest cultural traditions of the ancient Near East. In order to understand the "law of the messenger"[3] it is necessary to remember that ancient societies (and some contemporary ones) had no means of rapid communication. Travel from place to place took days or weeks. People lived without telephone, telegraph, radio or mail service. Under those conditions, situations naturally arose where a person needed to be, but physically could not be, in two places at once. A king could not be in his palace, at the court, leading his armies in a war, and conducting peace negotiations with another enemy all at the same time. A businessman could not operate an establishment in Jerusalem and at the same time buy or sell wares at the port of Jaffa. And so on. Thus, early in the cultural history of the ancient world a practical solution to this dilemma was developed. A person could not be in two places at once but a person could authorize another person to serve as his agent in one or more of the necessary places. Since those agents could not pick up the phone and check on details with their principals, the agents were on their own in conducting the mission.

Thus, all that was needed for the use of a commissioned agent was a task that needed doing somewhere that the ruler, owner or other principal could not be. Kings commissioned ambassadors and envoys. Merchants commissioned business representatives. King David even wed Abigail through an agent. In his *Embassy to Gaius* the Jewish philosopher Philo tells of being commissioned as an envoy to the Roman Empire by the Jewish community of Alexandria. Striking new evidence of how old and important the system was has now been found in the famous Ebla excavation in Syria. In the more than twenty thousand clay tablets that have been discovered, there is one business report after another of the commercial agents of that city, which flourished from 1800 to 2500 B.C. The practice of commissioning agents was a vital part of the civilization of the entire ancient Near Eastern world.

In the history of the Jewish faith this common custom had been carried over to an application in religious matters. Representatives of Yahweh, both angels and people, were thought of as God's sent ones. The messenger prophets especially shared this idea. Isaiah heard, "Whom shall I send, and who will go for us?" and answered, "Here am I! Send me" (Isaiah 6:8). Jeremiah heard, "Do not say, 'I am only a youth';/for to all to whom I send you you shall go,/and whatever I command you you shall speak" (Jeremiah 1:7). The earliest church made use of the principle of agent to understand the apostles ("sent ones") who were believed to have been commissioned to special tasks by an experience of the risen Lord. So the world of John's day was marked by the widespread use and application of the law of the messenger. John describes Jesus nearly sixty times as one "sent from God." How far did he go in applying the messenger model to Jesus?

The Principles of the Law of the Messenger

In all its ancient forms and even in its use today in the practices of diplomacy, power of attorney and proxy voting, a few basic rules govern the law of the commissioned representative or sent one.

I. *Either separating distance or special circumstance requires that the problem be dealt with in an indirect way.* (When one party travels overseas, for instance, that party can give another the power of attorney to conduct business matters for the traveler at home.)

II. *The sent one is to be regarded as the sender in the performance of the mission by those with whom he must deal.* (That is why the takeover of the U.S. embassy in Teheran was such a serious affront, for by the legal definition an embassy and ambassador are an extension of their country.)

III. *The authority of the sent one is solely for the performance of a specific task or tasks and the sent one must obey the sender's instructions.* (An attorney who is authorized to complete the sale of a client's home may not decide to throw the client's car into the bargain.)

IV. *The sender grants the sent one full rights of representation, even to appear in court in the sender's stead.* (So in today's legal system, many civil and divorce cases are handled entirely by designated attorneys.)

V. *The sent one must return and report to the sender and turn over whatever property is involved.* (Failure to do so will result in legal action against the agent.)

VI. *The sent one, while equal to the sender in the performance of the mission, is always subordinate to the sender.* (Thus, a U.S. ambassador fully represents the President to another country, and is to be received and dealt with as the President would be in official matters, but the ambassador is always servant of the President.)

With these simple rules in mind, John's Gospel can be examined more completely to see how he modeled his new view of Jesus on this principle of the sent one.

John Applies the Law of the Messenger to Jesus Christ

I. *Jesus is God's envoy from heaven.*

The Evangelist goes to some length to illustrate the compelling need for a genuine representative from God. He begins that emphasis in the revision of the prologue. It concludes, "No one has ever seen God; the only Son, who is in the bosom of the Father, he has made him known" (1:18). (See also 6:46.) Jesus is, for John, the only one of God's representatives to come directly from God. John sees a gulf set between the heavenly realm of God and our existence on earth. He uses a number of images to describe that separation: God is above and we are below (8:23); God is in heaven and we are on earth (13:1); where God is we cannot go (7:33f). No other representative from God is therefore adequate, because none has come "from God": not Moses, not the prophets, not even John the Baptist. Both the necessity for God's self-revelation in Jesus, the sent one, and the uniqueness of Jesus as compared to all other messengers are established for John by this emphasis. Some passages that illustrate this theme in the Fourth Gospel include:

> If I have told you earthly things and you do not believe, how can you believe if I tell you heavenly things? (3:12).

> No one has ascended into heaven but he who descended from heaven, the Son of man (3:13).

> For I have come down from heaven, not to do my own will, but the will of him who sent me (6:38).

> If God were your Father, you would love me, for I proceeded and came forth from God (8:42).

II. *Jesus, the sent one, is equal to the Father, to the sender.*
One striking feature of the Fourth Gospel's portrayal of Jesus is the bold assertion of the equality of Jesus and God. It is not just a charge made against the Johannine Jesus by the opponents, though it is that (see 10:33f, 5:18). Jesus himself repeatedly makes the assertion that he and the Father are one. The most famous text is 10:30, "The Father and I are one."[4] For the Evangelist, to encounter Jesus is to encounter God. Some other examples of this dramatic theme in the Fourth Gospel are:

> If you knew me, you would know my Father also (8:19).

> And he who sent me is with me; he has not left me alone, for I always do what is pleasing to him (8:29).

If I am not doing the works of my Father, then do not believe me; but if I do them, even though you do not believe me, believe the works, that you may know and understand that the Father is in me and I am in the Father (10:37-38).

He who believes in me, believes not in me but in him who sent me. And he who sees me sees him who sent me (12:44-45).

If you had known me, you would have known my Father also (14:7).

Believe me that I am in the Father and the Father in me (14:11).

This Johannine theme of the equality of Jesus and the Father, found nowhere else in the New Testament, has formed the basis for many later debates about the nature of Jesus Christ, that is, Christology. This will be discussed later. Here it is important to note that in this Gospel Jesus is presented as God's sole representative, to be received as equal to God.

III. *Jesus is commissioned by God to perform specific tasks.*

No aspect of the Johannine presentation is illumined more clearly by the law of the messenger than that of Jesus being sent to perform a mission. The familiar, and probably pre-Johannine, traditional sentence of 3:16, "For God so loved the world that he gave his only Son, that whoever believes in him should not perish but have eternal life," has been restated by John in the next verse in terms of the mission of the sent one: "For God sent the Son into the world [cf. chap. 1:14-18], not to condemn the world, but that the world might be saved through him." Throughout the Gospel John makes it clear that Jesus' primary mission is to bring salvation. He does so by doing the works of God, by speaking the words of God, by receiving those given to him by God, and by glorifying God always. It is in these terms that the Evangelist spells out the specific tasks of Jesus as God's envoy.

A connection with the Gospel's roots in the Signs Gospel tradition is evident here. The promise of a coming prophet like

Moses, from Deuteronomy 18:15, continued in an important way for the Evangelist. Deuteronomy 18:18-19 restated the promise and went further:

> I will raise up for them a prophet like you [Moses] from among their brethren; and I will put my words in his mouth, and he shall speak to them all that I command him. And whoever will not give heed to my words which he shall speak in my name, I myself will require it of him.

Where the Signs Gospel had stressed the Mosaic-prophet theme focusing on the signs and wonders, John refocused it to stress the message of Jesus as the promised prophet who will speak God's word. The thorough way in which the Evangelist spells out the mission of the sent one is exhibited in the following illustrations:

> For he whom God has sent utters the words of God (3:34).

> For the works which the Father has granted me to accomplish, these very works which I am doing, bear me witness that the Father has sent me (5:36).

> For I have come down from heaven, not to do my own will, but the will of him who sent me (6:38).

> My teaching is not mine, but his who sent me (7:16).

> But he who sent me is true, and I declare to the world what I have heard from him (8:26).

> For judgment I came into this world (9:39).

> I came that they may have life, and have it abundantly (10:10).

> No one takes it [my life] from me, but I lay it down of my own accord. I have power to lay it down, and I have power to take it again; this charge I have received from my Father (10:18).

> The Father who sent me has himself given me commandment what to say and what to speak (12:49).

This repeated emphasis on Jesus' mission and on the tasks assigned to him by the Father, occurring often with the sending terminology, shows that the Evangelist was applying the analogy of the law of the messenger to Jesus.

IV. *Jesus, the sent one, is given full authority to complete his mission.*

Although this theme can be seen at several points in the Gospel, its expression is strongest in the affirmation that Jesus has been granted full authority to overcome both the hostile world and the evil one in gathering those whom the Father has given to him. It occurs as early as 3:35, "The Father loves the Son, and has given all things into his hand." Other passages also illustrate John's application of this part of the law of the messenger directly to Jesus:

> The Father judges no one, but has given all judgment to the Son (5:22).

> For as the Father has life in himself, so he has granted the Son also to have life in himself, and has given him authority to execute judgment (5:26-27).

> All that the Father gives [to] me will come to me (6:37).

> And this is the will of him who sent me, that I should lose nothing of all that he has given me (6:39).

> Yet even if I do judge, my judgment is true, for it is not I alone that judge, but I and he who sent me (8:16).

Thus Jesus is portrayed by John as possessing and giving life, as having the power to execute judgment and as having the power to receive the property of the Father. Jesus, in John's view, is the fully authorized representative able to act in God's stead.

V. *Jesus reports and returns to the Father.*

The return of Jesus and his report on the mission show John's most creative adaptation of the messenger model. Early in the story Jesus says to his disciples, "I shall be with you a little longer, and then I go to him who sent me" (7:33). The theme of Jesus' impending departure grows stronger as the Gospel proceeds.

> Now is my soul troubled. And what shall I say? "Father, save me from this hour"? No, for this purpose I have come to this hour (12:27).

> The hour has come for the Son of Man to be glorified (12:23).

> . . . When Jesus knew that his hour had come to depart out of this world (13:1).

> I go to the Father (14:28).

> And now I am no more in the world, but they are in the world, and I am coming to thee (17:11).

In the Fourth Gospel the cross does not represent the tragedy that it does in the other Gospels. It is the triumphant return of the sent one to the sender. That is why the Johannine Jesus says calmly on the cross "It is finished" rather than any cry of despair. Mission accomplished, Jesus is returning to the one who sent him.

Under normal circumstances of the messenger law, the report of the agent follows the return to the sender. But that normal sequence is a problem for the Evangelist. If he has Jesus wait to report until he has returned to the Father, then the separation of heaven from earth, which is the basis of the model, would prevent the disciples (and John's readers) from knowing what the report said. John's solution to the dilemma is clever. He has Jesus deliberately report out of sequence for the disciples' (and his readers') benefit. That report is found in chapter 17.

The prayer in chapter 17 is not a "High Priestly Prayer," as it is often called. Instead, it is a carefully constructed report by Jesus to the Father on the completion of his mission and a prayer for its successful continuation by the church. In 17:4 Jesus says, "I glorified thee on earth, having accomplished the work which thou gavest me to do." The following verses from chapter 17 specify the completed work:

> I have manifested thy name to the men whom thou gavest me out of the world (v. 6).

> I have given them the words which thou gavest me (v. 8).

> While I was with them, I kept them in thy name . . . I have guarded them (v. 12).

> I have given them thy word (v. 14).

In verse 13, the unusual circumstances of this report are even acknowledged: "But now I am coming to thee; and these things I speak [while I am] in the world, that they may have my joy fulfilled in themselves." This prayer is filled with sending terminology. It brings to completion John's creative application of the law of the messenger to an understanding of Jesus. Through this preview of the report to the Father, John's readers share full knowledge of the mission of Jesus, the sent one. Thought of in this way, the report prayer of chapter 17 adds poignancy to the farewell in 14:27, "Peace I leave with you," for "peace" (*Shalom* in Hebrew, *Eirene* in Greek) was and is the standard word of greeting and farewell in the Near East.

VI. *Yet Jesus remains subordinate to the Father.*

It is difficult to imagine a more exalted portrayal of Jesus than that given by John. Jesus certainly takes on trans-human, if not superhuman, characteristics in the Fourth Gospel. He possesses foreknowledge about himself and others. He knows the life story of a woman he meets for the first time at the well of Sychar. He can claim greater longevity than Abraham: "Before Abraham was, I am" (8:58). As the *Word* he was present at creation. He and the Father are one. John's revision of the Gospel dramatizes an exalted figure.

In spite of this indisputable heightening of the understanding of Jesus, John remained true to the model from which he was working. The Evangelist is careful to insist time and again that Jesus is *not* the Father and that Jesus, the commissioned one, remains subordinate to the Father. In fact, the famous equality text, 10:30, "I and the Father are one," follows the sentence, "My Father, who has given them to me, is greater than all, and no one is able to snatch them out of the Father's hand." Other passages firmly attest to the Father's real priority over the sent one:

> I can do nothing of my own authority (5:30).

> When you have lifted up the Son of man, then you will know that I am he, and that I do nothing on my own authority but speak thus as the Father taught me (8:28).

> And I will pray the Father, and he will give you another Counselor, to be with you for ever (14:16).

> If you loved me, you would have rejoiced because I go to the Father; for the Father is greater than I (14:28).

> But I do as the Father has commanded me (14:31).

The Johannine portrait of Jesus would be flawed without this emphasis. As the one sent, Jesus must remain subordinate to the will of the sender, God. John's faithfulness to this part of the law of the messenger shows us how thoroughly he was working with that principle as his model for Jesus. The later world of Christian debate about equal natures, three persons in one, etc., is completely foreign to the thought patterns of this great early Christian thinker. For that reason, as shown later, John's portrait of Jesus, the one sent from God, is an offense to almost any later Christian explanation of Jesus.

VII. *The Johannine Jesus also commissions the disciples.*
John extended the model by having the sent one send others. No concrete evidence in the secular use of the law of the messenger shows that an agent could deputize others in the completion of the mission, although it seems likely that practical necessity would have caused it to happen. At any rate, the extension is not an invention of the Evangelist. The idea is encountered in the other Gospels as well. "He who receives

you receives me, and he who receives me receives him who sent me" (Matthew 10:40, cf. Luke 10:16). That idea is crucial to the Evangelist Matthew's view of the church. Moreover, as noted earlier, the noun *apostle* ("sent one") was the word reserved for those few who were commissioned by Jesus in resurrection appearances (1 Corinthians 15:1-11). For John this idea of the commissioning of the disciples (the church) is vital. Jesus, sent from God, extends that commission to the disciples. Examples are:

> We must work the works of him who sent me (9:4).

> Truly, truly, I say to you, he who believes in me will also do the works that I do; and greater works than these will he do, because I go to the Father (14:12).

> As thou didst send me into the world, so I have sent them into the world (17:18).

> That they may all be one; even as thou, Father, art in me, and I in thee, that they also may be in us, so that the world may believe that thou hast sent me (17:21).

> As the Father has sent me, even so I send you (20:21).

This theme is the functioning heart of John's message. The portrait of Jesus as the one sent by God leads the reader to the bold conclusion that the disciples are equally commissioned ones. The high view of Jesus (Christology) ultimately results in an equally high view of the church (ecclesiology). With this final identification the author has made the mission of Jesus, and the mission of the church in his own day, one and the same. That cannot be overemphasized in understanding the Fourth Gospel. This is why the Signs Gospel was revised. John freely overlaps the life of the church of his day with the life of Jesus in the expansion of the Signs Gospel. He had really begun the revision for the purpose of restating and renewing the faith of the church of his day. He had done so by drawing an unbreakable link between the present life of the church and the life and mission of Jesus. He makes the tasks of Jesus the tasks of the church of the present. The plain fact is that the

Johannine Trinity consists of Father-Son-Disciples (the church) and the Spirit is only an adviser. So the story has come full circle. The Gospel of the sent one is the Gospel of and for the sent ones!

One further result of the sending model's domination of the Fourth Gospel should be pointed out. Scholars have long puzzled over why the discourse in chapter 14 ends with, "Rise, let us go hence" (v. 31), and yet no one moves until three chapters later, at the beginning of chapter 18. Since chapters 15 and 16 seem to repeat and rethink the content of chapter 14, some have thought that the confusion was caused by the later insertion of all of chapters 15, 16 and 17 by a later editor. But that would eliminate the report to the Father, which is vital to the Evangelist's portrait of Jesus. Moreover, chapter 17 has little or nothing in common with chapters 15 and 16. However, once it is realized that first-century Jewish people prayed standing, the mystery clears. Jesus says, "Rise, let us go hence." They rise. He offers a final prayer, chapter 17, and they go out (18:1). The sequence is really natural but has been blurred by the insertion of chapters 15 and 16 by the later editor and by the failure to follow the messenger model's use in John.

Thus it is fairly certain that the Evangelist wrote the bulk of the revisions of the Signs Gospel now found in John 1-20, minus the later addition of chapters 15 and 16. It was a remarkable achievement that succeeded in its own day and proved to be so intriguing a restatement of the faith that it has had an immeasurable influence on subsequent Christian thought. No matter how badly it has been misinterpreted by later generations, who viewed it through the lens of their times and cultures, the Gospel of John's graphic portrayal of Christ and the Christian mission stands as one of the great seminal works of the faith.

Suggested Supplementary Reading

The best treatment of the messenger model is in the work of Peder Borgen. Most accessible is a chapter on the subject in his book *Bread for Heaven*.

For a good study on Christian use of the sending idea in connection with apostleship see C. K. Barrett, *The Signs of an Apostle* (Philadelphia: Fortress Press, 1972).

Questions and Suggestions for Study

1. Underline all the places where "send" occurs in John. Does the occurrence of this word correlate with the author's proposition that this is a dominant theme in the Gospel?

2. What are some modern uses of the law of the messenger?

3. What aspects of John's application of the messenger model are exciting to you? What aspects are troubling? Why?

4. Does the Johannine "bottom line," so to speak, "As the Father sent me so also I send you," do anything to alter your previous views of this Gospel? What?

9

Summary of the Work of the Evangelist and the Final Redaction

From the introduction of the prologue, to the expansion of the Signs Gospel story of the healing of the man born blind into a drama of faith, and on through the fascinating use of the messenger model for the portrayal of Jesus, this book has followed John at work. The new Gospel is so forceful, its portrayal of Jesus so striking, its message so strong that it is not hard to understand why it has been such an important Christian document. Judged by almost any standard, even by those who deeply dislike the Johannine version of faith, it is the work of genius.

But it is a special genius. This Gospel exhibits the virtues of simplicity. In its language, in the message and in the choice of topics, John has stayed with the relatively simple, the repetitive, the memorable. The language of this Gospel, especially of John, is simple, slightly Semitic Greek. There is no wealth of vocabulary. The grammar is simple and straightforward. And that simplicity is maintained in the subject matter. Time after time, in section after section, the Evangelist repeats and stresses ideas that have already been presented. Concepts echo and re-echo through this work in a haunting way. John must have known more about the Jesus tradition that he used. Perhaps even the Signs Gospel was reduced. He chose to reinterpret his community's faith through concentration on a few themes and stories rather than by treating everything. There, too, the choice of simplicity was effective. The early Christians were mainly common people. Though the author is well versed enough to use the Old Testament in a technically precise way in chapter 6, he did not turn to technical argument to make most of his points. He revised the Signs Gospel so that it spoke with simple elegance directly to the problems that confronted his people in their day and time. Even as misread as it certainly has been by subsequent Christian generations, it has served many of them well, too, as a fountainspring of faith and understanding.

The concluding chapter will begin a probe of the Gospel's relevance for our day and time. Here the important new light that current research has thrown on the Evangelist's achievement must be reemphasized. Every religious tradition, and especially the Christian tradition, lives in a constant tension between reverence for received tradition and the need for reinterpretation suited for the life of a new age. Some think that this process began with the eighteenth-century enlightenment in Europe and the rise of critical thinking in the Western world. It is true that since that time the tension has been acute, but it did not begin then. The process of reinterpreting tradition had begun in the first century, and it was given its sharpest impetus by the radical changes that the Jewish War had caused. Matthew, Luke and John (and I believe Mark also) were all involved in the task of rethinking the faith for the new days of the last part of the first century. Students of Paul rewrote Colossians, and then wrote Ephesians, for the same purpose of renewing a faith tradition. The success and vitality of this reinterpretation process did much to help the Christian faith survive those troubled times.

So the discovery that John does not repeat the words of Jesus, that he even sharply revised the tradition about Jesus which he had received (the Signs Gospel) should not be shocking. Instead, today's readers should begin to put themselves in John's times and observe his efforts to help make living sense of a deeply troubled faith, sensing the burden which pressed him on in his venture of reinterpretation. He and his fellow Christians must almost have wept by the waters of Babylon. They had been cut off from the synagogue, their spiritual home. So John reached deep into that past tradition of the promised Messiah/Prophet, into current religious ideas and to familiar secular culture, to recombine and recast the gospel message for his new day. That effort at empathetic appreciation helps today's readers understand John. Such empathy is vital to a fair reading of any ancient work.

It would be surprising if any reader of John today, or of this study, could simply nod assent to everything the Evangelist wrote. He did not write for our time or for our problems. But if his work is looked at through the discoveries of the new research, his revision of the faith statement can be followed with fascination. Our own situation can be reassessed and this great Christian work can be used in a new and positive way, discovering times when it is pertinent to today's faith issues and when it is not.

The Final Edition: The Addition of Chapters 15, 16 and 21

The present state of this Gospel suggests that John's revision of the Signs Gospel was a success among the Christians for whom it was written. In fact, the existence of the Epistles of John, also written in and for this community and also reflecting revered use of John's work, gives ample reason to think that his work was readily received. By the first decade of the

---

A Model of John's Work as Evangelist

The Resources:
The Signs Gospel
The Hymn-Poem to the Logos

The Situation:
Christians are being expelled from the synagogue.
The "Signs" faith is no longer working.

The Tools of Reinterpreting:
The Drama/Dialogue technique.
The Synagogue Sermon form.
The Model of the "Sent One."
John's own theological perspective nurtured in his Christian
Jewish heritage.

The Result:
John 1—14, 17—20--a dramatic new portrait of what
Christian faith means.

---

second Christian century, John's revision probably had replaced the Signs Gospel as those communities' primary testament of faith.

In the next decades, however, the use of the Johannine Gospel itself prompted questions and controversy. As a result, the Gospel underwent further revision before it became widely known in the manuscripts now available. The separation from Judaism had become complete, a thing of the past, and both life and faith now focused on living as Christians in the world outside the synagogue. That new situation again called for some rethinking of the message, as had the situation in John's day.

This revising process, although it is uncertain whether it was completed by one person or in stages, is encountered in the expansion of the final discourse of chapter 14, by the addition of chapters 15 and 16, and in the appended section, chapter 21. One of the first clues to the revision and its purposes comes in the discussion of the subject of the Paraclete, or

Counselor. John had presented Jesus as saying in 14:16-17: "And I will pray the Father, and he will give you another Counselor, to be with you for ever, even the Spirit of truth. . . ." And he repeated the message later in verse 26: "But the Counselor, the Holy Spirit, whom the Father will send in my name, he will teach you all things. . . ." Apparently this message about the Spirit, which John clearly wrote in retrospect, was a difficult one for the Johannine churches. Note that the tenses alternate between future and present in verse 17 because John and his church already knew the Spirit which Jesus was promising. In 15:7, 26 and 16:26, the later editor both clarifies and contradicts what has been said by Jesus in John's revision.

As discussion of the role of Jesus in the faith proceeded in these communities, there was a concern to enhance and enlarge the role of Jesus. So the editor insists, in spite of John's explicit statements, that the Spirit will be sent by Jesus and not by the Father. John could not do that, nor would he have wanted to do so, because of the sending model. Jesus could and did commission the disciples, but only the Father can send a heavenly representative. But the editor does not perceive, or else does not feel bound by, the Johannine sending analogy, and heightens the role and authority of Jesus by having Jesus send the Spirit.

Why didn't the editor just revise chapter 14? Why bother to add material that is so blatantly contradictory? The reason for this is reflected in much of the early Christian (and Jewish) attitude toward tradition. John had not felt free to ignore the Signs Gospel tradition. Tradition was too important to these people. Instead he had altered its meaning by adding material to it. In the same way, the later editor is not free to directly revise John's work because it is revered by the community. He must add material which makes the intended point. That is troubling. It caused difficulties for the later church in its attempt to develop a coherent doctrine of the Holy Spirit. But it did not trouble the early Christian writers and readers. The editor meant for his new, explicit statements in chapters 15 and 16 to overshadow and override those aspects of chapter 14:

"But when the Counselor comes, whom I shall send to you from the Father . . ." (15:26) and, "If I do not go away, the Counselor will not come to you; but if I go, I will send him to you" (16:7). The editor even has Jesus deny that he will pray to the Father, as stated in 14:16. The glorified Christ doesn't need to do this. He is one with the Father, and the Father already loves the disciples. It is not difficult to follow the editor's reasoning here, or to see that in this reasoning he is beginning to abandon the sending model.

In addition to that editorial revision, the editor(s) chose to emphasize, even more than John, the commandment to love one another. The famous line "Greater love has no man than this, that a man lay down his life for his friends" (15:13) suggests that the editor is concerned for communal loyalty even to the point of martyrdom. Sporadic Roman pressure against Christians was beginning in those decades (John of Patmos was exiled about A.D. 96; Ignatius and Polycarp were martyred about A.D. 110), and some Christians may have lost their lives in the synagogue dispute. The increased stress on community loyalty is easily understood. The same emphasis is encountered in 1 John 2:7-11 from a writer of the same circle and probably the same era. This is a glimpse of the Johannine church under new fire, now from the Romans as well as from the synagogue; and in 1 John, at least, one senses a danger of division and schism within the community. The church was entering a dangerous new time and Christians needed to be reminded of the command to love one another.

Yet just as John had done in his revision of the Signs Gospel, so the editor (and the author of 1 John) is satisfied to allude to other commandments of Jesus, presumably well known in the community, to which the readers are called (15:10, cf. 1 John 2:3). Once again it is the stress which is important. For the Evangelist, the later editor and the author of 1 John, the life of the community was seen to hinge upon their loyalty to and compassion for one another. Without that loyalty and compassion in those times of peril and persecution, the tensions could spell the end of the community of faith.

Whether the same or another editor added chapter 21 is difficult to say. In some aspects the appended chapter is farther away from the work of the Evangelist than either the addition in chapters 15 and 16 or the work of the writer of the first epistle.[5] It differs sharply in language, subject and mold. Only the exchange between Peter and Jesus in 21:15-19 has a Johannine ring in its repetition and misdirection. So while the stage at which the appendix was added is uncertain, some things are discoverable about what the attachment of chapter 21 accomplished for the one who appended it and for the readers.

The first moderating influence or stress in chapter 21 may be seen in the geographical focus of the unit. The Signs Gospel and John's revision had concluded with the resurrection stories that centered around Jerusalem. Just as in Luke's Gospel, the disciples did not flee in terror or despair to Galilee after the crucifixion but remained in Jerusalem. The encounters with the risen Christ occur in that context. In John 20, Jesus appears first to Mary Magdalene and then in the upper room to the Twelve and especially to Thomas. Yet another early tradition located the primary resurrection appearances in Galilee. In fact, these Galilee appearances appear to be the only ones which Mark and Matthew know or care to tell. By adding chapter 21 to the Fourth Gospel, an editor sought to find a middle way and to avoid division and controversy among Christians over that issue. Now this Gospel contains stories of the appearances in both Jerusalem and in Galilee. Since no indication is given in this addition that the editor wants to deny the validity of the Jerusalem appearances, as Luke explicitly denies any outside Jerusalem, the purpose must be to affirm both resurrection traditions and to avoid conflict on an issue which the editor does not believe to be important.

Another striking feature of the Johannine appendix chapter is its emphasis on Peter. Even though Peter does play a role in John's Gospel, it is a far less important role than the one he plays in the other Gospels. There, especially in Matthew and

Mark, Peter stands out as the chief spokesman for the disciples and the prototypical disciple in faith, in doubt and even in denial. In John 20, in a section probably derived from the Signs Gospel tradition, Peter is outraced to the empty tomb by the "other disciple" (v. 4), and is thus only the second witness to the empty tomb among the disciples. The winning "other disciple" is "the one whom Jesus loved" (20:2). Neither disciple is mentioned again after that incident. Clearly one cannot say that Peter's role is pre-eminent in the Fourth Gospel. His importance is even deliberately played down, with him taking second place to the beloved disciple.

What is this all about? Why the fuss over who won the race to the tomb? This probably shows a blurred glimpse of some problems of authority and loyalty among early Christian groups. The Jerusalem Christian church, at least until A.D. 70, gave primary loyalty to James, and then Jude, who were of the family of Jesus. That is, they organized themselves under the leadership of the dynasty of Jesus, the Messiah-King. Other churches gave primary loyalty to Peter. The famous passage about the keys of the Kingdom, in Matthew 16:18-20, is one clear indication of a community with Petrine allegiance. Paul also expected loyalty from the churches he founded. Much of the controversy between Paul and the Corinthian church revolved around the validity of his apostolic leadership. Inevitably these loyalties clashed. Johannine Christianity did not trace its origins to a mission by Peter but to the work of the unknown beloved disciple. Cast from the synagogue, these Christians were forced into primary associations with other Christian groups. John had acknowledged this in his revision of the Signs Gospel, on the periphery of his concern, by the allusive comment of 10:16, "And I have other sheep, that are not of this fold; I must bring them also, and they will heed my voice. So there shall be one flock, one shepherd." The Johannine community had a living concern for the unity of the diverse Christian communities.

By the addition of a chapter in which Peter is given a leading role, indeed one in which he is told repeatedly to "tend my sheep" (21:15-17), the editor sought to join together the Petrine mission and strand of early Christianity and the Johannine strand. This is one of the earliest examples of the drive for Christian unity, just as the much earlier Jerusalem encounter between Paul and the leaders of the Jerusalem church had the same intention.

The First Letter of John shows us that division among Christians was a dark cloud gathering itself in these early years of the second century: "They went out from us, but they were not of us; for if they had been of us, they would have continued with us; but they went out, that it might be plain that they all are not of us" (1 John 2:19). Even without knowing who "they" were, these words illustrate the pain of the early Christian schism. Working as a force in the opposite direction, toward Christian unity, the editing of John's Gospel to include the appendix chapter was done to avoid such splits and splinters into sectarian opposition. The editor still honors the memory of the founding of the community by the beloved disciple but not in such a way as to exclude honoring the apostolic work of Peter. So simple an addition may have meant very much to Christians of both groups and gone a long way toward ensuring wider acceptance for the Fourth Gospel in the whole church.

Finally, a rather obvious appeal to authority is made in the concluding verses of chapter 21. "This is the disciple who is bearing witness to these things, and who has written these things; and we know that his testimony is true" (v. 24). This verse must come from the hand of the editor because of the tell-tale "and we know that his testimony is true." In that sentence the disciple is thought of in third, not first, person. The beloved disciple could not have written that sentence. It is the work of the editor. Why would he make this assertion? Unless it is just a casual comment, in which case its stress at the closing is odd, the reference to apostolic authority here must mean that some Christians were already challenging the reliability and validity of the Fourth Gospel.

A moment's thought about the nature of the Gospel story in Matthew, Luke and Mark (all of which were written by the editor's day and were growing in use and popularity, especially Matthew) shows that it is a short step to challenging the Fourth Gospel's validity. Some must have done so. The new conclusion to the Gospel, in verses 24-25, is a slightly wistful attempt to assure the readers that the Fourth Gospel is a valid Gospel. The editor accounts for the uniqueness of the account by asserting that there is much else about Jesus that has never been told (v. 25). This clever conclusion may have aided the Fourth Gospel's acceptance in the wider church just as did the new inclusion of Peter. The same kind of ascription to Paul of letters in Ephesians and in the Pastoral Epistles is further evidence of the reliance on apostolicity to verify a writing's worth. But today, with the knowledge that none of the Gospels can be read as an accurate historical portrayal written by actual disciples of Jesus, this appeal to authority may be found quaint and overstated, as though the editor protests too much.

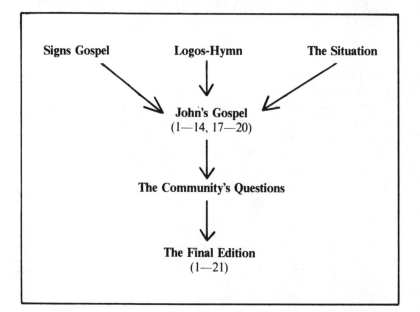

With the editor's work, the story of the shaping of the Fourth Gospel comes to an end. In the second quarter of the second century the texts of all four Gospels became largely set. They were widely circulated among Christians all over the Empire. The process of direct revision to meet new faith crises was at an end. From then on such reinterpretation was done through commentary and sermon. These Christian writings were well on their way to being chosen as scripture by the orthodox churches of the fourth century. Yet in the Gospel of John are clues which help unravel its story and enable readers to follow the process by which it came to be. Biblical scholarship in our time has largely succeeded in reading those clues and in bringing this Gospel's fascinating story to light. From the early, somewhat simplistic Signs Gospel, through the brilliant revision by John, to its final editing and adaptation in the early second century flows the faith story of an early Christian community. It was continually confronted by the problem, "What does the Gospel mean in this new day?" Perhaps the witness of this story can lead to reflection on that question for our time.

Suggested Supplementary Reading
Not much is written about the work of the final editor, but a good deal has been written about the Epistles of John, whose origins are similar. The best introduction to that study is the recently published commentary on the Johannine Epistles by R. E. Brown, *Anchor Bible*, Vol. 30, completing his work on John for that series. An older but especially valuable treatment is that by the British scholar C. H. Dodd, *The Johannine Epistles* (London: Hodder & Stoughton, 1946).

Questions and Suggestions for Study
1. Compare carefully the comments about the Paraclete in chapter 14 with those of chapters 15 and 16. Do you see the changes the editor made? Note them.

2. Read chapters 20 and 21 in succession. Note that no transition is provided between 20:31 and 21:1. Why didn't the editor eliminate 20:30-31 or save it for the final conclusion?

3. Read 1 John. Do you notice the curiously repetitive style of argument? Did John use the same technique to a lesser degree? Do you think this letter could be the work of the Evangelist? Why or why not?

10

The Gospel of John and Faith in Our Time

The new wave of research on the Gospel of John leads to far greater understanding and accuracy about how the Gospel came to be. It is now apparent that the *good news* was shaped and reshaped by and for early Christian Jews who were struggling to make their faith relevant to new situations. This new view of John is, of course, valuable for its own sake because by it a fuller understanding of this ancient document occurs. But that is not the only value in a reappraisal of the Fourth Gospel. The new view opens doors for our own rethinking and appropriation of the Christian faith.

Especially since the provocative ideas of Rudolf Bultmann became widely known in the 1950s, a great deal has been written and said about Christian interpretation of the Bible—hermeneutics. Bultmann argued that the message of the New Testament must be demythologized because it presupposed a view of reality which was no longer shared. Some recoiled at the idea that any part of the biblical message was out-of-date. Some wished to insist on the historical reality of at least some part of the message; for example, the resurrection of Jesus. Others went far beyond anything Bultmann had ever dreamed of in *secularizing* the Gospel. A recent wave of criticism of the historical-critical study of the Bible says it is too pedantic, sterile and lifeless. Some, notably in Old Testament studies, are calling today for appreciation of the Bible as the church's canon, as a whole, and not in terms of what it meant to the original writers and readers. And, of course, there has been, is and probably always will be the popularizing reading of the Bible which assumes that the actual meaning of the text does not matter; it is only what one gets out of it when reading it now that matters. So the issues of reinterpretation are in ferment today.

Can the new view of the Gospel of John provide some clues about the interpretation and use of the New Testament? It can in a number of important ways. First, all the research upon which this new understanding is based begins from a single imperative. A person honestly studying a biblical book wants to know and needs to know what the writing meant to the writer(s) and to the original readers. No matter how difficult and intimidating that task is, that first level of understanding needs to be established. There is no other control over biased speculation, flagrant misinterpretation and abuse of ancient writing, particularly a religious one. Those arguing today against historical-critical analysis because it is sterile, and who propose psychological or sociopolitical or even imaginative (structural) norms in its place, are all guilty of seeking to impose *their* meaning on the texts rather than being willing to let Isaiah or John or Paul say what they had to say.

No credible alternative to seeking, as far as it is possible, to find and follow the communication between the original writer(s) and readers exists.

But that is only a first step. Leaving the matter there puts the painstaking critical recovery of the story safely away on the dusty shelf of an archive. Having established the original communication between the writer and intended readers, a contemporary reader will ask, even if subconsciously, "So what? What does this message, from and for a time long ago, mean for me today in my life?" Raising that question causes a movement from the historical reconstruction of the content to the question of contemporary relevance. It is, or ought to be, an inevitable step. What the new view of the Fourth Gospel does is to show that exactly that same process was part and parcel of the formation of the Bible itself. The Fourth Gospel is the model and example here, but it should be understood that the Gospel of John is unique only in the thoroughness of its reappraisal of past tradition. Every one of the Gospels, the book of Acts, the Pauline and Deutero-Pauline letters, and the book of Revelation can all be shown to have undergone the same process. The writers of all these books, sometimes through several stages of writing, took up and rethought earlier tradition in order to give it new meaning for a new time.

To be specific, the writer of the Signs Gospel chose from among available traditions about Jesus, then ordered and edited them so that they could serve his readers as a testimony to their faith in Jesus the promised Messiah/ Prophet. He did *not* simply repeat the actual story or stories of Jesus, but he formulated the tradition so that it could proclaim faith for his day. Later, in the community where the Signs Gospel was now popular, John took it up and boldly revised it to give a *new* meaning for the new issues confronting the church in his day and time. The process did not even end there. John's Gospel was then re-edited by another Christian (or Christians) from that continuing faith community so that it would deal with the problems of the church of an even later date. Careful reading can reconstruct much of that fascinating process. It becomes the story of the Fourth Gospel.

Taking note of this raises the question, What is the relationship between received tradition and contemporary life in any age? Writing about the problems of the church in Asia, Bishop Nirmal Minz of the Evangelical Lutheran Church in India says:

> Second hand and derived theological thought cannot take a church too far in its life in a given environment. It must spring out of people's life situation. Until its theology is the struggle of the church in a given situation in the proclamation of the Gospel, a church will remain isolated from the situation with an alien vision of Jesus Christ.[6]

That fact is much clearer in a mission situation where cultures must be transcended than it is where a faith is a dominant cultural assumption, but the process must always go on, or the tradition will cease to have meaning for anyone. The Fourth Gospel gives vivid illustrations of the process very early in the life of the church.

The Signs Gospel presupposed a Jewish religious foundation for the new Christian faith. It was written in and for a community of people who interpreted their faith as a fulfillment of the messianic hopes of Judaism. They were secure in that context and evangelistic in that setting. But then the setting blew up. The Jewish War brought chaos and altered Jewish society radically. In the ensuing struggle with Pharisaism for supremacy, the Christians lost out and were ejected from the synagogue. The Signs Gospel was then made irrelevant because the situation it presupposed and addressed no longer existed. In the midst of that crisis, the Evangelist John came forward with a radical reinterpretation of the Signs Gospel. He expanded it to speak directly to the people of his day in drama, dialogue and sermon. He redrew the portrait of Jesus so that, as the only one sent from God, Jesus overshadowed Moses, Abraham and the prophets. He turned the readers' attention away from miraculous works as proof of Jesus' Messiahship to the message of his sent Christ as the center of faith. To the members of the Johannine churches the revision came as a new call to a new identity. It renewed and restored the community's faith. Even the final, later editing of the Gospel shows clear evidence that it was undertaken only because there were new problems that the later community faced which were not adequately dealt with in John's revision. It needed refinement to deal with the new issues of their time.

Thus, the Gospel of John is the result of early Christians conscientiously adapting their faith to new days. That is an inevitable, necessary task. It is one of the most exciting challenges for people in every age. The new view of the Gospel of John calls upon today's readers to do precisely the same thing for this time. The call is to move forward from the biblical heritage, rooted in that heritage, to restate the faith for this day. This does not mean mere repetition of the Bible's message. That is religious stagnation, which misunderstands the Bible itself. Which message should be repeated? Jesus' message? The Signs Gospel message? John's message? The final editor's message? All of them at once? It becomes an absurd question. But the Gospel of John and all biblical tradition can be used both as model and resource as the faith is restated in new terms for this day.

A contemporary example of that process at work illustrates that it is happening now. In the last generation, the great theologian Paul Tillich struggled to restate what he believed to be the heart of the message of Paul and Luther. His reformulation goes, "Accept the fact that you are accepted, in spite of the fact that you are unacceptable."[7] The sentence struck a deep chord in many people's minds. Today it is so common a way of describing God's gracious approval that speakers and writers often do not even know, or need to acknowledge, that the phrase was Tillich's. A new way of saying something old, yet vital, about the faith had been found that appeals to our time. The process has gone on *in* every age with any vitality *for* every age with any vitality.

The Fourth Gospel, and especially the example provided by the Evangelist, lets his rethinking for his age trigger rethinking on some issues that confront this age. What task confronted John? The Signs Gospel faith had lost much of its meaning in the environment of that time. Expelled from the synagogue community, the foundation beliefs of the Christian community were called into question. Pressures from Judaism and from the Gentile. world threatened to destroy the little Christian group entirely. Their future seemed bleak. The situation was grave.

What are some features of the environment which confronts the church in current times? A faith largely derived from the nineteenth-century world has been the faith of this dramatic century of change. Most hymns, prayers and orders of worship (especially in Protestantism) have been taken over from that time. The expression of faith ranges from creeds like the so-called Apostles' and Nicene Creeds, which are steeped in the problems of the church in their days, to some modest efforts to restate the faith in more modern terms, such as the Korean Creed, the Presbyterian Confession of 1967, etc. But the key crises of this generation have not been adequately addressed. This age has vaulted from the horse and buggy and Model A into the Space Age, an age of nuclear power, largely urban population, mass communications systems and startling advances in medicine. The dizzying pace of change is both a delight and dilemma.

Much more importantly, the basic elements of understanding the world and ourselves have changed. The view of Greek dualism, both in the world of mind and matter and in the human as body and soul, is vanishing in our time. This view had dominated Western thought for fifteen hundred years. But the natural science which made technological progress possible is more and more monistic. The universe, incomprehensible and old beyond imagining, is still a closed energy system. Every part of it, from subatomic particle or wave and the electrical impulses which create mind and ideas, to the vast stars and nebulae, is part of one great system of energy ($E=mc^2$) in marvelous diversity. That science does not need to presuppose an external creator God, and for practical purposes does not do so. Religious people and groups may fight against it, but in laboratory and classroom, in business and government, in medicine and agriculture, this view grows stronger and more secure each day. More poignantly, it also applies to human beings. It is not just a matter of the theory of evolution, although sophisticated understanding of that process is also part and parcel of our world. It is even more a matter of the great new discoveries in genetics (i.e., the RNA/DNA complex that is at the root of all organic life), in medicine, and in neurophysiology. More and more this culture operates with the view that a human being is a mind-body unity. Thus in both the outer and inner worlds, the traditional Christian presuppositions are threatened.

At the same time the world experiences rapid social change. Communities, families and work relationships have altered dramatically in the past forty years. New attitudes about what constitutes personal fulfillment, an increasing stress on material values, and widespread challenges to some traditional moral values all are signs of the times. The church's dilemma is that, like the church of John's day, it has brought its theological formulations and moral principles along from another, and now vastly different, age. Its ethics enshrine some past set of values, depending on the particular heritage, but the church has generally been slow to respond to its changing world. Especially in the areas of family life, divorce and sexuality, the new age produces a crisis of values. The undergirding rationale for the old values has been deeply shaken by societal change, medical advance and greater individual freedom. Traditional male-dominated structures are threatened as women break out of those roles which were accepted everywhere until a generation ago.

Confronted with that world, the church is in crisis. Science and learning are no longer fighting some of the old cherished faith presuppositions; they have simply moved beyond the argument. Many people find the church outdated, even among those who remain basically loyal. Young people, in particular, sense the widening gap between the church and the world and "turn off" the church. Few people in the United States today act and think as though their Christian faith were the center of their lives.

Consideration of John's solution to his crisis may be of some help in finding a solution to today's crisis. When the Signs Gospel faith had faltered, both theoretically and practically, he undertook to revise that faith so that it could speak for his day. With the old Jewish anchors torn away, John sought to convince the readers that the abiding significance of Jesus could stand on its own. Moreover, he deliberately overlapped the story of Jesus' day and that of his own. He also solved the problem by projecting for his readers an image of Jesus as sent by God. Finally, he called the church to new life by equating its mission with that of Jesus.

How many of these Johannine solutions can be appropriated for the current situation? Virtually none of John's great ideas can be transplanted without reinterpretation to the church of the twentieth century. But only one of them is probably impossible. John had the audacity to tell the Jesus story (or at least use the Signs Gospel as Jesus story) and his church's story as though they were one, and felt free to move back and forth in verb tenses and pronouns as he did so. Though it might be an interesting project for a church to attempt that today, it would not sit well as a way of restating the faith. It would not do because of the possible misrepresentation of Jesus. It is difficult enough to recover Jesus' original message in the parables and sayings without compounding it by mixing then and now.

But the other Johannine solutions, critically appraised, could help. First, John's model attacks the faith question of his time head on and not on the periphery. The problem for his day was the conception of God, of Jesus' relationship to God and of the church's relationship to both. That is today's prob-

THE GOSPEL OF JOHN

lem, too. A way to give answers that are appropriate to the world in which today's readers live, as John did for his world, must be found.

All the strands of modern Christian faith are caught up in a dilemma at this point. Virtually every church tradition wishes to give a positive affirmation to the great Christian creeds developed in the church from A.D. 175 to 475. But every word of those creeds was shaped in a context, for a struggle and with a world view different from today. A good example may be seen in the Nicene Creed. Virtually no living Christian in the United States lives and thinks in the heavily philosophical, metaphysical framework which is the structure of that creed. Anyone who does has managed to skip the most rudimentary modern scientific view.

Actually, John's work may be at the root of our problem. In his exalted portrait of Jesus, John made Jesus more than human but less than fully divine. One with the Father in mission and even in heavenly origin, Jesus remained subordinate to the Father who was greater. In the debate behind the Nicene and Athanasian creeds, John may in fact be closer to the position of Arius, declared heretical, who held that Jesus was a half-God. But since all the Greek thinkers were interested in essence and nature, while John was interested in function and purpose, the use of John is out of kilter anyway. Nevertheless, all subsequent theology took the Nicene-Athanasian route of elevating Jesus to full divinity. So this tradition provides the definition of the Trinity and the conception of Jesus as truly God *and* truly man. But in that faith Jesus always loses his genuine humanity to the overriding claims of divinity.

In today's world, that point of view takes on the character of fantasy. Indeed, at times Christian apologists as diverse as C. S. Lewis and Billy Graham seem not to mind that they call their readers or hearers into a world of fantasy—for in fantasy everything is possible. But God as an austere external presence and Jesus as an incarnate divine-man are ideas that may be bankrupt today and for the foreseeable future, regardless of how well they have served long ages of Christian faith. Faced with that fact, there is a tendency to become defensive and to leap to the assumption that the Greek Trinitarian ideas are the absolute minimum for Christian belief. Thinking that way, however, makes unChristian practically every New Testament writer, including John. The early Greek philosophical formulations in the creeds are of the same character as John's revision of the Signs Gospel; they were an attempt to restate the faith in living terms for their day. That day is not our day. The task must be renewed.

Some signals in our time point toward new ways of expressing the faith. They may come from the impulse of the deepening awareness of creation's wholeness (ecology); from the widening awareness of human oneness in liberation movements including that of women; and in a growing sense that the ultimate is to be found not in an external realm or presence but at the center of existence, in the here and now, in the very stuff of which people and the world are made.

Look at the last point first. When John revised the Signs Gospel, one message of his Jesus was about the Spirit. Since then, that has always been read in the sense of a power from outside. But if one can be born, in John's image, by the power of the Spirit then the Spirit must be an experiential and immediate awareness. Even in our modern rat-race existence there are precious moments when a silence, a sound, or someone's special gesture touches to the depths. Those times are reminders that these depths of feeling, perceiving and response are possible and that they make life truly human. They are not just an echo of eternity, they are real eternal presence. "The hour is coming, and now is, when the true worshipers will worship the Father in spirit and truth" (John 4:23). Even religious language needs to move beyond repetition and jargon and into contact with the profound sense of rootedness, of oneness, of at-homeness, that is meant by John and is an ever-present possibility. When Paul Tillich spoke and wrote of ultimate concern, when Rudolf Bultmann wrote of authentic existence, and even when Dietrich Bonhoeffer wrote of religionless Christianity, all three were pointing toward this very real dimension of existence. When God is found at the center of existence as a nourishing, sustaining and challenging presence, and ways of expressing this are found which do not falsely turn God into an external idol, then perhaps a new way of stating theology for today is coming.

"For God so loved the world" (John 3:16). The Johannine definition of world needs to be revised. John meant the world of human beings. The hard facts of natural reality have created an ecological consciousness. Now it is apparent that unthinking, manipulative and exploitive use of the natural world will always rebound as loss, at best, and disaster at worst. Human beings are bone and sinew, nerve and fiber, mind and body, part of the created universe. So the faith must be rethought to take this strong awareness into account. John solved the dilemma of Christian exclusion from the synagogue by the ringing promise of Christian inclusion in the heavenly realm, "In my Father's house are many rooms" (14:2). Most subsequent Christianity has been like John in that respect. Gone is the earlier Jewish apocalyptic hope of the restoration of earth, "Thy will be done on earth as it is in heaven." Fervent apocalypticism had failed because the end did not come. And it isn't coming, either, in the way that radio and television preachers try to envision it or in Hal Lindsey's dramatic vision. The earth may die as an atomic cinder or as an ecological dump, but neither will represent the apocalyptic kingdom of God. For the sun will continue in its path, the stars to move in their orbits. Just as the focus needs to turn today to a search for the meaning of God at the center of life, so theology needs to redefine salvation so that it includes all of creation, for that is where God is at work. True salvation will be found only in nurturing, caring for, and cooperating with the earthly environment and even, someday, space. For in and through it all God is present. Focus on this perspective is done best today by theologians like John Cobb and Schubert Ogden, among others, who have recognized that theology must speak to the contemporary view of the world where all things are in process, interrelated and dynamic. So, too, they suggest thinking of the presence of God and of human beings in continual process, always changing, always in interrelationship with others and the world.

The most painful and difficult aspect of responding in faith by seeking God at the center and by recognizing God's presence in all of creation is the loss of the body-soul dualism. That hurts because it threatens the fond hope for immortality. Many Christians say they wouldn't be Christians without this promise, not even realizing how blatantly self-centered such a demand is. Just as John struggled to redefine faith for his day, when naive apocalyptic hopes were fading, so too must we redefine the present, vital and vibrant meaning of faith and salvation today, when the body-soul dualism and all that attends it is coming to an end. To be loved now by God, to be at home in God's universe, to participate in this given time and with loved ones in life's richness, and to be taken up eternally into God's memory—these are ways to think and speak of salvation. These are ways to honor the heritage that says salvation is more than just a good feeling without denying the reality of human finitude. At least they point in a direction that may help solve one of modern faith's great dilemmas.

The turn to liberation as a major theme in Christian theology corresponds to the Johannine focus on community. John was greatly concerned that the Christians of his community sense their oneness and that they also be open to oneness with others. This concern is marred in John's thought only by his sectarian hostility to the world and the Jews. Today's interpretation of that oneness needs to occur in more radical terms than John's; oneness means openness to all human beings. For John also believed that the way opened by Jesus was the way to real freedom. In our day, what does such freedom mean? It has to start with genuine, personal and social freedom and move to spiritual freedom in personal and interpersonal wholeness. That is why Christians cannot focus simply on the "spiritual" even though the Fourth Gospel is read in that way. Being born anew of the Spirit is not simply a religious and emotional experience that makes one somewhat obnoxiously smug about one's faith. For John it meant a reorientation of life toward God in Christ and toward others. In that light, the Christian faith must be the opponent of every social system, including pseudo-Christianity, which stereotypes and oppresses persons and denies them their full humanity.

God's love for the world, in John, meant all humanity. Thus today, attention to that faith means that a Christian not only cannot be a racist but must oppose racist structures everywhere—be it Chicago, Memphis or Johannesburg. It furthermore means recognition that all are God's children, though not all experience it or acknowledge it (cf. John 1:13), and sexism must also be opposed. There is no valid theological reason not to treat women simply and fairly as equals everywhere, especially in the church. God's love as seen in Jesus also means that Christians care about others who are poor and oppressed because God's intended potential for their lives is thwarted by economic, political and cultural deprivation. In Bombay, India, the shantytowns of the wretched poor clutter even the airport approaches. In Guatemala and much of Central and South America, Amero-Indians are forced to live in subhuman squalor. A faith that knows of the presence of God in and among all things cannot look at such degradation without heartache and without response. That concern for others cannot be overemphasized in any gospel for our day.

Then, too, John's stress on community should not be overlooked in the effort to restate the faith. His Christian community was faced with dissolution because of the radical shift in their world caused by the Jewish War. Moderate and liberal Christianity, both Protestant and Roman Catholic, may face a similar peril today. On one side a robust secular world calls people today to a life set free from the structures and burdens of the old religious orientation. It appeals to self-fulfillment and self-gratification in a barrage from advertising, the media, contemporary music, films and literature. On the other hand, conservative Christians appeal to people to forsake the world and join a rearguard action with a "hold the line" mentality.

Christian communities and persons reluctant to sell out to a self-centered secularism or modernism, but just as reluctant to turn to dogmatic, biblical literalist arrogance and ignorance with its repetition of worn-out creeds, doctrines and customs, are now hard pressed to survive.

John found two solutions to that dilemma—he framed a new Christology and a new doctrine of the church. Could they be keys for our time? Some elements of John's Christology are not credible for our time. The signs and miracles testimony to Jesus must be critiqued. Jesus viewed as "from above" or "from afar" is a motif which cannot carry its weight today. Taken literally, of course, there is no longer any "above" (where is up in an expanding, spherical universe?) or any "out there" from which Jesus could have been sent. It is better to stress the human reality of Jesus as one who pointed toward God and not toward himself. And the exclusivism of John's Christology, "No one comes to the Father, but by me" (14:6), is also problematic, especially in the light of its corresponding Christian arrogance toward others. It served John as a tool to combat Pharisaic exclusivism. It does not serve very well now and tends to lead into the sectarian exclusion of and belittling of others. So again the question must be asked, "How can the significance of Jesus for this time be expressed in a non-arrogant way?"

It seems unlikely that the creeds' concern about dual nature (divine/human) or triune divinity can have much value for today's world. Creative new insights about Jesus as the one who opens eyes to God's truth and presence, as one who calls people to live in that presence, as one who is a window to the divine, might help to restate the good news in a time when the heaven/earth dualism is no longer relevant. Concerns about who is a heretic, as though the faith were sealed in plastic in some past age, need to stop. Our minds must be set to rediscovering Christ for our time as John did for his.

But even if some elements of the Johannine Christology are deeply troubling, some aspects of his application of it to Christian life may yet spark fire. In John's view, God sent

Jesus who sent the church. In practice that means that whatever one says about the character and purpose of God, and the character and purpose of Jesus, is also an assertion about the character and purpose of Jesus' followers. Too bold? Perhaps. But the analogy deserves further thought. If God loves human beings and that love is revealed in Jesus, then does it not follow that the Christian must not only receive the love but hand it on as well? If God forgives and that forgiveness is encountered in Jesus then the Christian is not just forgiven but a forgiver. If God seeks salvation (wholeness) for all people and that seeking is encountered in Jesus, then Christians are not only made whole but are called to share in the seeking.

The church does not have to be dogmatic, arrogant or exclusive to take up this sense of destiny. Nor is it a uniquely Johannine idea. The same message flows through Matthew's Gospel, "You are the light of the world" (5:14). It is what Paul meant by lines such as "We are ambassadors for Christ, God making his appeal through us" (2 Corinthians 5:20). Modern Christians can take themselves and the mission of the Christian community seriously without having to don the offensive trappings of pseudo-evangelical aggressiveness and appeals to fear. Living as ones sent by God becomes a matter of consciously and clearly living out and speaking out for what the church believes.

And in this time of peril the Johannine emphasis on "Love one another" deserves more attention. It was no accident that Paul wrote the famous "love chapter" (1 Corinthians 13) to a church troubled by inner turmoil. Paul's "more excellent way" and John's "new commandment" are aimed at the same basic truth. Nothing about the Christian faith will be very convincing today if Christians do not live that faith in a simple, humble way—in personal lives, in the society—but especially in community with one another. Gone are the days in U.S. society when the church or parish was the automatic center and social unit for people. If Christians are going to live out their faith in the present time, they must find ways to care for, nurture, learn from, and love one another. Sectarian, separatist Christian groups have far outshone more moderate Christians in this respect. Perhaps John's community was being driven toward a separatist, sectarian mentality by its situation. But do Christians have to wall themselves in to be Christian? Do they have to fear the evil world? Do they have to deny the good in their culture in order to love one another? Surely not. If so, the love of which Christianity speaks is hollow, reserved only for the inner circle of fellow sectarians, and it is no model for abundant life.

Nevertheless, the level of commitment *to one another*, not to the church as an abstraction or institution, but *to one another*, is a measure of faithfulness. Outsiders sense that fact when they point to rank hypocrisy as a major flaw in the church. No Christian community will ever fully live out the call to love one another, but Christians committed to living the faith in and for this time need to renew the call to community as the anchor of all other efforts in mission, theology, education and worship. It is crucial that the new commandment, "that you love one another," be heard once more.

These are only a few issues that the Gospel of John can prompt for our time. Every reader needs to go beyond these to ask, "What are the urgent issues in the church and the world where I am, where we are?" For Christians must do the work of God who sent Jesus where they are now, in the face of the problems of this new day. What does the good news about God have to say about issues of family life, abortion, sexual practices, political concerns, the practices of worship, war and peace, and on and on? The Bible can come to life now when it is approached, not as lawbook or fixed creed, but as a witness to the living faith of others as they wrestled with the issues of those times. Then, and only then, its vivid example can prompt Christians today to get on with the task of living the faith for a new day.

Questions and Suggestions for Study

1. One Christian ethicist and theologian of our time is fond of saying that the problem with modern belief in God is that it is an oblong blur. Is that true? Where would you like to clear away the blur? Does reflection prompted by the Fourth Gospel help?

2. What practical ways can be employed to help Christians "love one another" in our day?

3. What problems and solutions do we encounter in repicturing the significance of Jesus for today?

11

Conclusion and Reprise

This study began with an awareness that renewed interest in religion and the Bible was both a blessing and a dilemma for the church today. The bombardment of voices calling for a literalist interpretation of the Bible has increased and found sympathy from even the current U.S. President. At the same time, that point of view is held up to ridicule in other portions of society as a prototype of narrow-mindedness, authoritarianism and unthinking dogmatism. When the battle lines are so joined there seems to be no place for a sensitive person to stand, with integrity, between mindless literalism and sneering skepticism. This survey of the new view of John has shown that there is a far better, more faithful and more intellectually honest way to read the Bible than either of those extreme alternatives.

I can vividly recall an event from my childhood in a small town in rural Iowa. When I was twelve, a teacher discovered that I had miserably failed a quiz on fractions that she had written on the board. It was not that I had done the problems on my paper wrong; it was that none of the problems I had written down matched what she had written! A sensitive teacher, she kept me out of recess the next day for a vision test. I was badly nearsighted and needed glasses. That was a damaging blow to the ego of an active and athletic Midwestern youth. Yet the day my glasses arrived and I put them on is a day never to be forgotten. It was a marvelous experience. I stepped out of the house and looked at my world, so familiar, with astonishment. The trees that yesterday had been a gentle green blur now actually had individual leaves and branches. I wandered about in amazement drinking in that new visual perception. And from that day I have never been embarrassed about my glasses. They are my window to a truer, sharper, much more accurate picture of the world.

The same process of sharpening discovery can take place in our relationship to the biblical books. For some people the books of the Bible, read in a naively literal way, are very familiar and yet, somehow, blurred of meaning. For others the difficulties encountered in believing what is said in parts of the Bible, because of the clashes with modern science and culture, have alienated them from the biblical works altogether. From either type of nearsightedness, the steadily progressing discoveries of biblical research can free today's readers so that the gentle blur becomes an exact and fascinating story and the clashes become understandable and less offensive. The new view of the Bible traces the crises, the hopes, the solutions and the faith of people wrestling with the world they encountered. In the biblical writings, new stories are discovered within stories of how the books themselves came to be. In their story and content is challenge after challenge to participate in the same process in our time, to think through the faith issues for our day in creative ways, as the biblical writers did for their times.

Once this bridge is crossed, our sense of loss at no longer being able to view the Bible as the infallible *words* of God fades away, just as my youthful embarrassment over eyeglasses, to be replaced by a joyous new encounter with a biblical world and a story of real people engaged with human dilemmas not unlike our own. Now the living Word of God is encountered, not enshrined in a past but vital and alive in our midst and time. Those seeking to live out a faith for a new day also encounter the Spirit of truth. If the example of the study of the Fourth Gospel, probably today's most exciting case, can entice readers over that hurdle and fit them with new lenses for seeing God's truth, then once more this great book of the Bible becomes a Gospel, the good news, urgently needed for lives today.

Every step in the writing of the Fourth Gospel was a step of reinterpreting the tradition in the light of problems from a new life situation. The writers used creatively the resources of emerging Christian tradition, the Old Testament, the worship and traditions of Judaism and the wider culture. In each case—Signs Gospel, John's great revision, and the final editing—the new perspective boldly adapted it to a new environment. This fresh view of the Fourth Gospel offers the challenge to this same bold task for today. The Christian faith can live for Christians at this time if the best of what has been received is taken up and reapplied with creativity and imagination to the needs of this time. In teaching that important process, in revealing the Gospel of John's fascinating story, the new view of John becomes a precious resource in a time when it is sorely needed. For like the Evangelist, a new day of great peril and great promise is at hand.

Suggested Supplementary Reading
On the issue of biblical interpretation the best and simplest work may be that of the British scholar James Barr. See both *Fundamentalism* (London: SCM, 1977) and *The Bible in the Modern World* (London: SCM, 1973). See also L. Keck, *Taking the Bible Seriously* (Nashville: Abingdon, 1979).

A next step in discovery could be an inquiry about a similar new view of Paul and his letters. See C. Roetzel, *The Letters of Paul: Conversations in Context* (Atlanta: John Knox, 1975); L. Keck, *Paul and His Letters* (Philadelphia: Fortress Press, 1979) and V. Furnish, *The Moral Teachings of Paul* (Nashville: Abingdon, 1979).

Questions and Suggestions for Study

1. What issue or problem is troubling you and your community right now? What resources from the Christian faith might apply?

2. What element(s) of the Johannine view(s) of Jesus are troublesome for you now? Why? Are there ways to resolve the tension?

Notes

1. J. L. Martyn, *History and Theology in the Fourth Gospel* (New York: Harper and Row, 1968), p. 36.
2. See, for example, R. E. Brown's *Anchor Bible.*
3. H. Rengstorff, *Theological Dictionary of the New Testament* (Grand Rapids: Eerdmans, 1964).
4. The Revised Standard Version "I and the Father are one" is unduly arrogant and ungrammatical. The translation given here follows R. E. Brown, *Anchor Bible*, Vol. 29, *The Jerusalem Bible*, and others.
5. Few critics today think that 1 John was written by the Evangelist who revised the Signs Gospel, but it comes from the same circle and uses many of the same terms and ideas to deal with a later situation.
6. In R. P. Beaver, ed., *The Gospel and Frontier Peoples* (Pasadena: William Carey Library, 1973), p. 109.
7. This phrasing is found at several points in Tillich's published works. See, for example, *Systematic Theology*, Vol. 2 (Chicago: University of Chicago Press, 1957), p. 179.

A Brief Annotated Bibliography

(Current works on the Gospel of John available in English)

Borgen, Peder. *Bread from Heaven.* Leiden: E. J. Brill, 1965.
    Though this study is quite technical, it is the best available treatment of the Johannine homily in John 6 and its roots in first-century Jewish homiletic interpretation of scripture. Here, too, Borgen gives the reader a glimpse of the importance of the sending theme in the gospel.

Brown, Raymond E. *The Community of the Beloved Disciple.* New York: Paulist Press, 1979.
    This little volume draws together the results of the author's research on the Johannine literature by sketching his view of the stages of the community's development. In some ways this view may be too bold in sketching too much complexity, and in some ways too conservative in viewing the historical origins of the community; but it is one of the best sketches that we have of the possible stages in the development of Johannine Christianity: its concerns, its crises, its stresses and its developing faith.

_____ *The Gospel According to John.* The Anchor Bible, Vols. 29 and 29a. New York: Doubleday, 1966 & 1970.
    The great two-volume commentary is one of the finest resources in all of biblical scholarship. Raymond Brown treats the Gospel with encyclopedic care as well as bold interpretation.
    Particularly valuable to the inquiring student of the Fourth Gospel is the introductory section. All the issues in date, sources and authorship are fully explored, the alternative theories discussed, and the author's judgment on them given with care and clarity.

Bultmann, Rudolf. *The Gospel of John: A Commentary*, trans. by G. R. Beasley Murray. London: Blackwell, 1971.

Bultmann's classic commentary is largely responsible for the explosion in Johannine research in the last generation. Until 1971 it was available only in German, and so was not available to many American readers. The commentary is noted for its bold hypotheses about the sources that lie behind the gospel and for the thesis that it is deeply influenced by Gnostic thought. Not many follow Bultmann's ideas today, but the reader can see how provocative his approach was and how it led to further, corrective research.

Dodd, C. H. *The Fourth Gospel.* Cambridge: Cambridge University Press, 1968.

This is the most important of a trilogy of works on the Gospel of John by the great British scholar. It is valuable in terms of both its treatment of the great themes of the Gospel and its commentary-like treatment of the argument and structure of the Gospel. Dodd represents perhaps the last attempt to see the Gospel from a strongly Hellenistic point of view. Most more recent studies have viewed it in a more strongly Jewish context. Nevertheless, the learning and insight in this book provide a great resource for any student of the Gospel.

Kysar, Robert. *The Fourth Evangelist and His Gospel.* Minneapolis: Augsburg, 1975.

For the reader who would like a review of the interpretation of the Gospel of John from Bultmann to the present, this book provides an excellent, balanced discussion. The author has a clear eye for the important contributions of a multitude of scholars and provides us with a very helpful review of the literature.

_____*John, the Maverick Gospel.* Atlanta: John Knox Press, 1976.

Written as a brief introduction to the Gospel of John, this little book introduces the reader to some of the key ideas and the uniqueness of the Fourth Gospel. The author has some difficulty in condensing material into clearly readable sections and some readers may find the going difficult, but this is a book intended to help the nontechnical reader encounter the Gospel.

Martyn, J. Louis. *The Gospel of John in Christian History.* New York: Paulist Press, 1979.

This collection of essays carries on the author's quest for the historical backdrop of the Gospel. It consists of three separate essays. The most helpful section for the nontechnical reader will be the final essay, which charts Martyn's view of the history of the Johannine community. A reader can easily set it alongside that of Brown (see above, *The Community of the Beloved Disciple*) and make some comparisons and contasts.

_____ *History and Theology in the Fourth Gospel.* New York: Harper & Row, 1968.

Here is one of the most important New Testament studies in the last fifty years. With the skill of a craftsman in historical reconstruction, Martyn takes the reader step by step through the process of discovering the setting of the writing of the Gospel. The analysis of John 9:1-41 is classic and the argument that the expulsion from the synagogue took place under Gamaliel II is presented here with careful support. Anyone seriously interested in the new view of the Fourth Gospel needs to consider this work.

Smith, D. Moody, Jr. *Johannine Christianity.* Columbia: University of South Carolina Press, 1984.

Professor Smith has spent most of his career working on John's Gospel. He has been particularly interested in the question of the Gospel's sources, and the essays in this volume bring the reader up-to-date on the discussion of that important question. Anyone who wants to think through the evidence for a "Gospel of Signs" will be helped by this study. The concluding essay is an excellent reflection of the theological and religious significance of the study of the Gospel of John.

Correlating Faith for a New Day with the Common Lectionary.

In the columns below are listed the texts from the Gospel of John that are used in the Common Lectionary, the pages from *Faith for a New Day*, and the Sundays on which they are the lectionary readings.

Texts from John's Gospel	Page No.	Cycle A 1987, 1990, 1993, 1996, 1999	Cycle B 1988, 1991, 1994, 1997, 2000	Cycle C 1982, 1992, 1995, 1998
1:6-8	36f., 40	Additional Lessons for Christmas	3rd Sun. of Advent	
1:1-14	16, 18, 36-40			
1:1-18	16, 18, 36-40. 69	2nd Sun. after Christmas	2nd Sun. after Christmas	
1:19-28	20		3rd Sun. of Advent	
1:29-34	20	2nd Sun. after Epiphany		

1:35-42	20			2nd Sun. after Epiphany
2:1-11	20		2nd Sun. after Epiphany	
3:1-17	50, 60, 70, 71	2nd Sun. of Lent	Trinity Sunday	
3:14-21	60, 71		4th Sun. of Lent	
4:5-26	50, 60	3rd Sun. of Lent		
6:1-15	48-50		Sun. between July 24 & 30	
6:24-35	50-54		Sun. between July 31 & Aug. 6	Thanksgiving Day
6:35, 41-51	57f.		Sun. between Aug. 7 & 13	
6:51-58	53-55		Sun. between Aug. 14 & 20	
6:55-69	50-55		Sun. between Aug. 21 & 27	

9:1-41	42-47	4th Sun. of Lent		
10:1-10	58, 72		4th Sun. of Easter	4th Sun. of Easter
10:22-30	70-76			
11:17-45	58-67	5th Sun. of Lent	All Saints' Day	
12:20-36	74	Tues. in Holy Week	5th Sun. of Lent & Tues. in Holy Week	Tues. in Holy Week
13:31-35	62			
14:1-14	58, 71, 77	5th Sun. of Easter		5th Sun. of Easter
14:15-21	61, 78, 83-84	6th Sun. of Easter		Pentecost
14:23-29	75, 84			6th Sun. of Easter
15:1-8	84		5th Sun. of Easter	
15:9-17	85-86		6th Sun. of Easter	
15:26-27	84-85		Pentecost	

Reference	Psalms			
16:4-15	85			
16:12-15	85			Trinity Sunday
17:1-11	67, 74, 75	7th Sun. of Easter		
17:11-19	74, 75, 77		7th Sun. of Easter	
17:20-26	77			7th Sun. of Easter
18:1 — 19:42	78	Good Friday	Good Friday	Good Friday
20:1-18	87	Easter	Easter	Easter
20:19-31	15-21, 24, 77, 91	2nd Sun. of Easter	2nd Sun. of Easter	2nd Sun. of Easter
20:19-23	77	Pentecost		
21:1-19	86, 88-89, 91, 86			3rd Sun. of Easter
21:15-19				

Index